SUPERHERO

Cut and Coloring Books™

SUPERHERO Cut and Coloring Books 3

Published by Cut and Coloring Books, LLC.
Lansing, Michigan

First edition October 2018

ISBN: 978-0-9995343-3-5

Printed in the United States of America.

Cut and Coloring Books.

is a complete partner with

NH Design Firm.

WARNING

Be careful of sharp objects aroud eyes

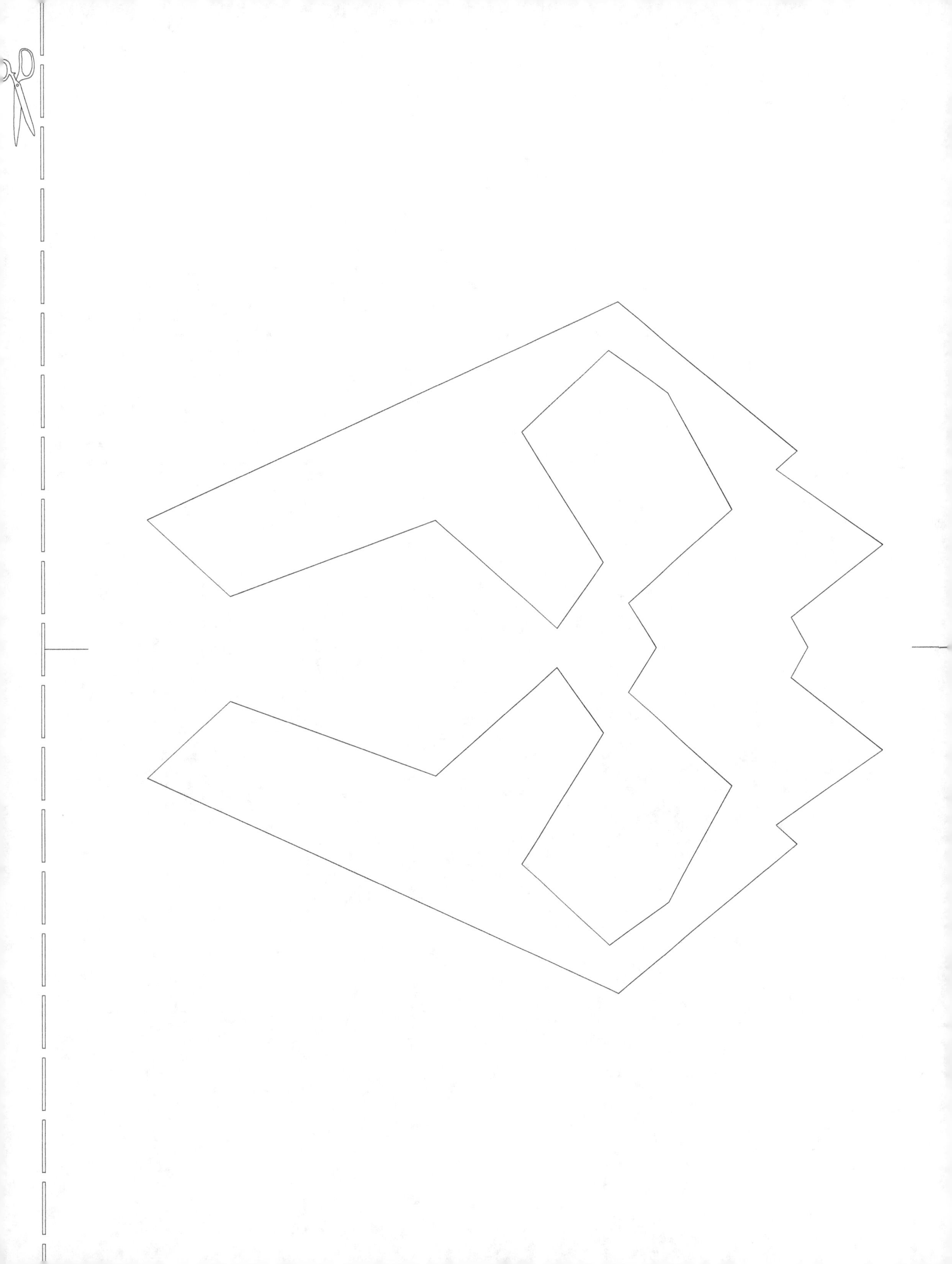

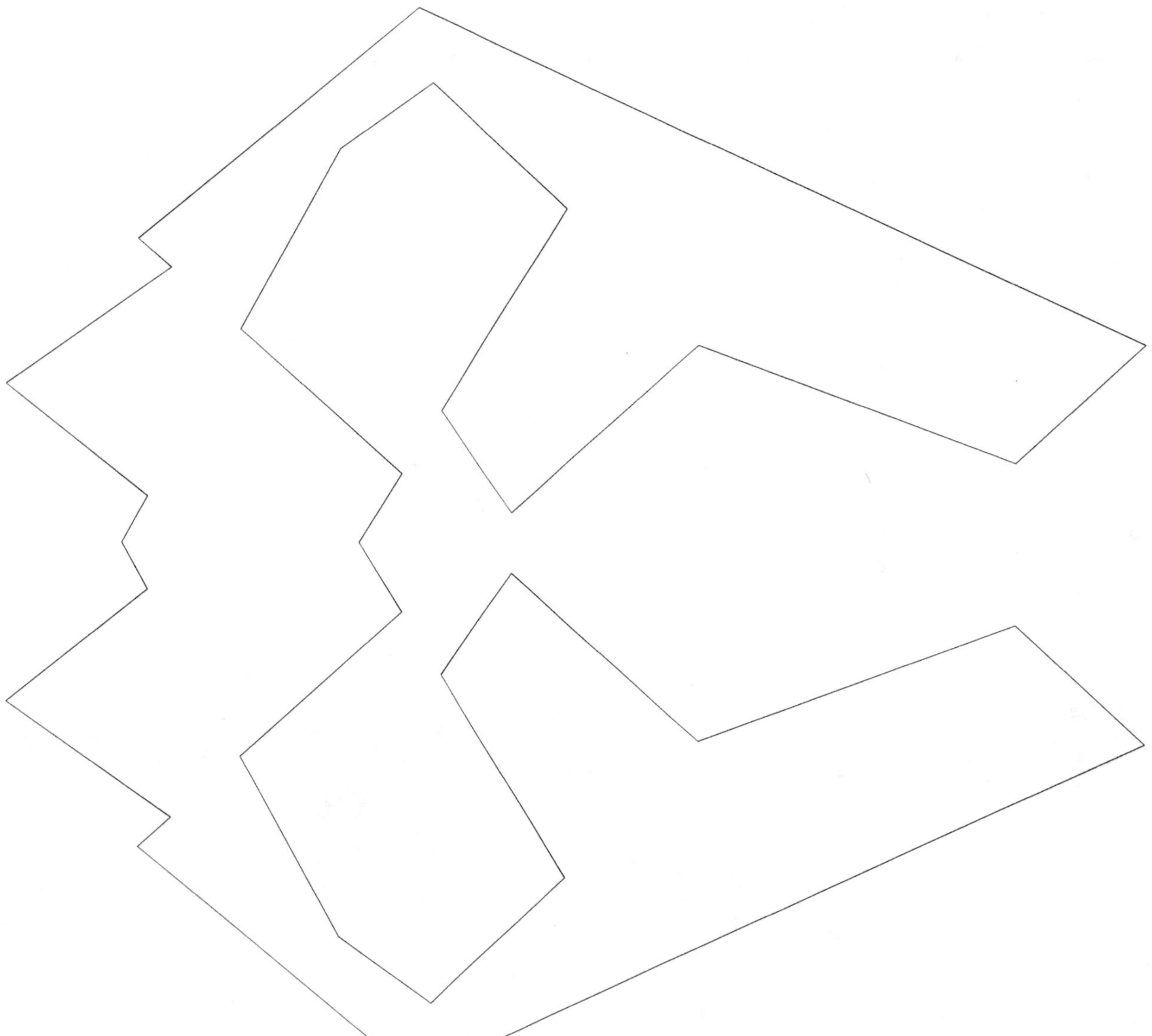

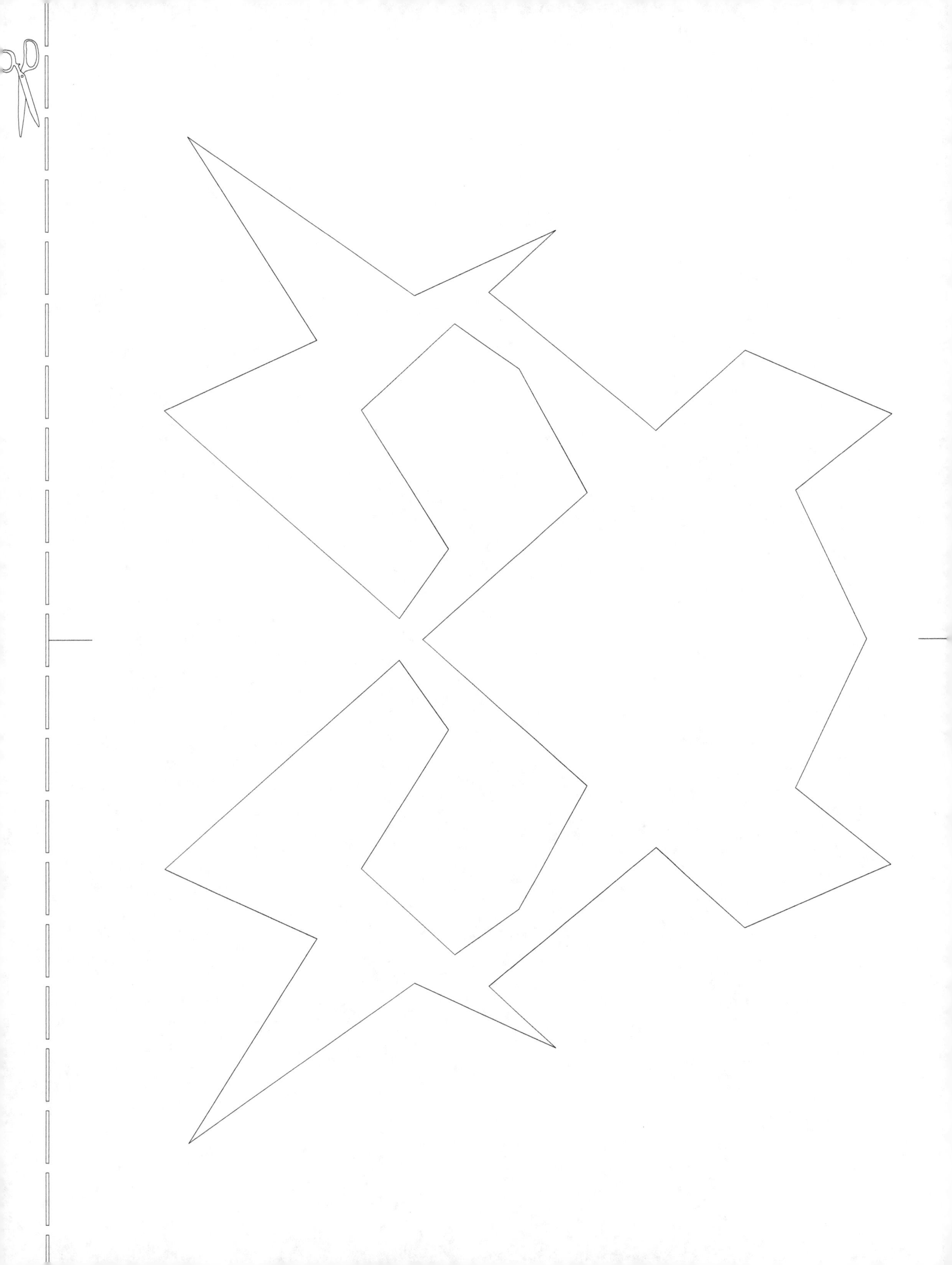

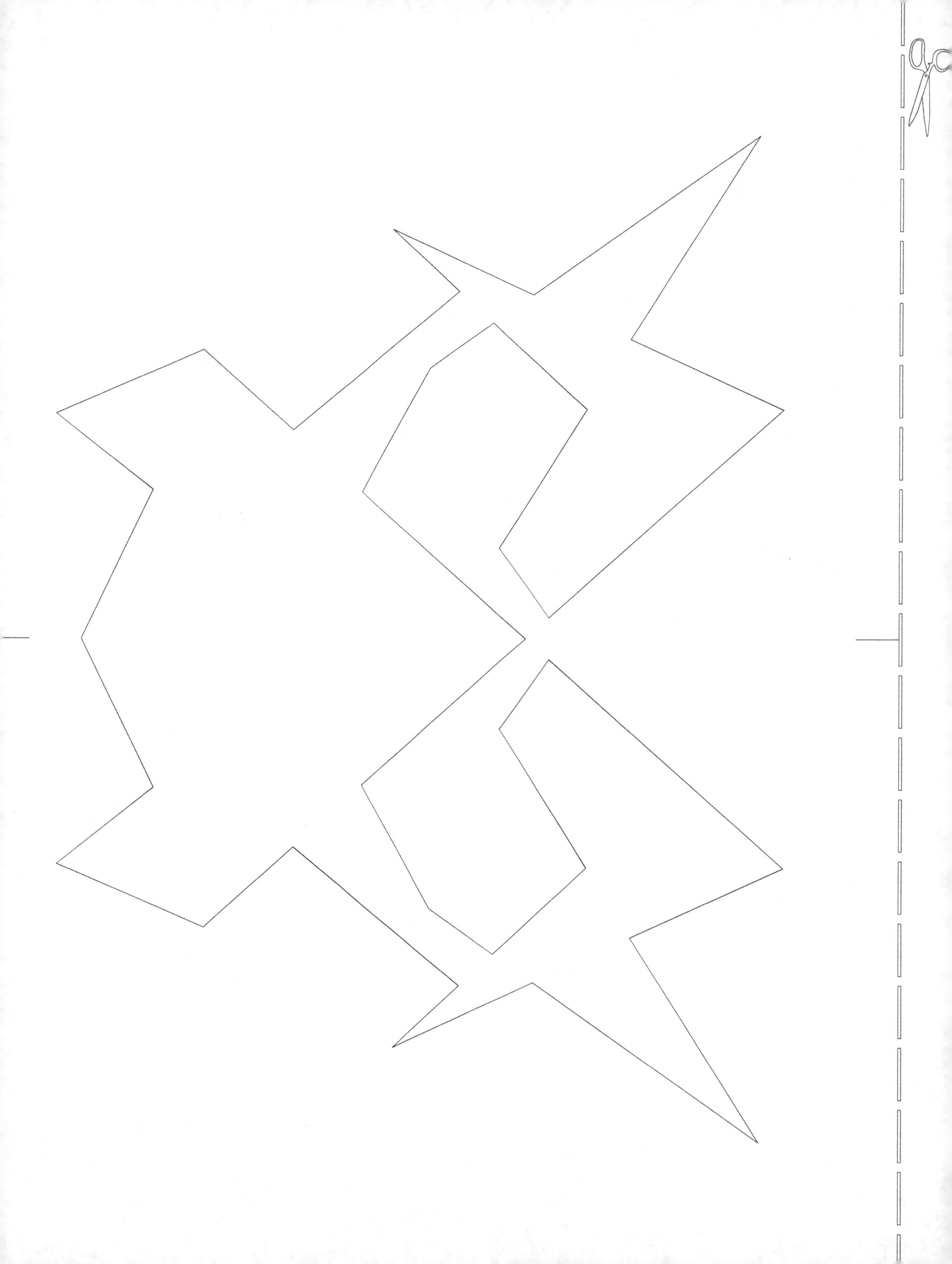

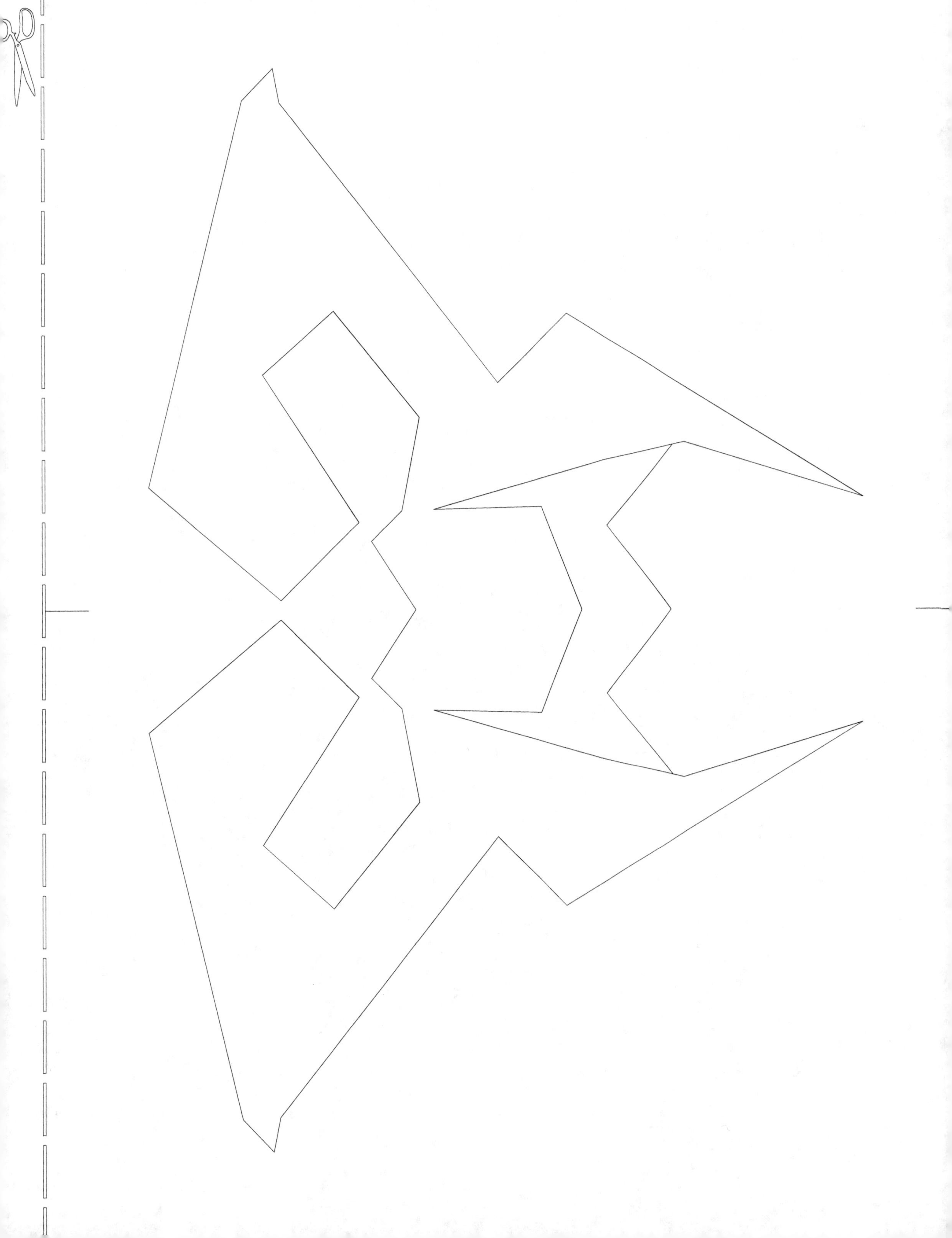

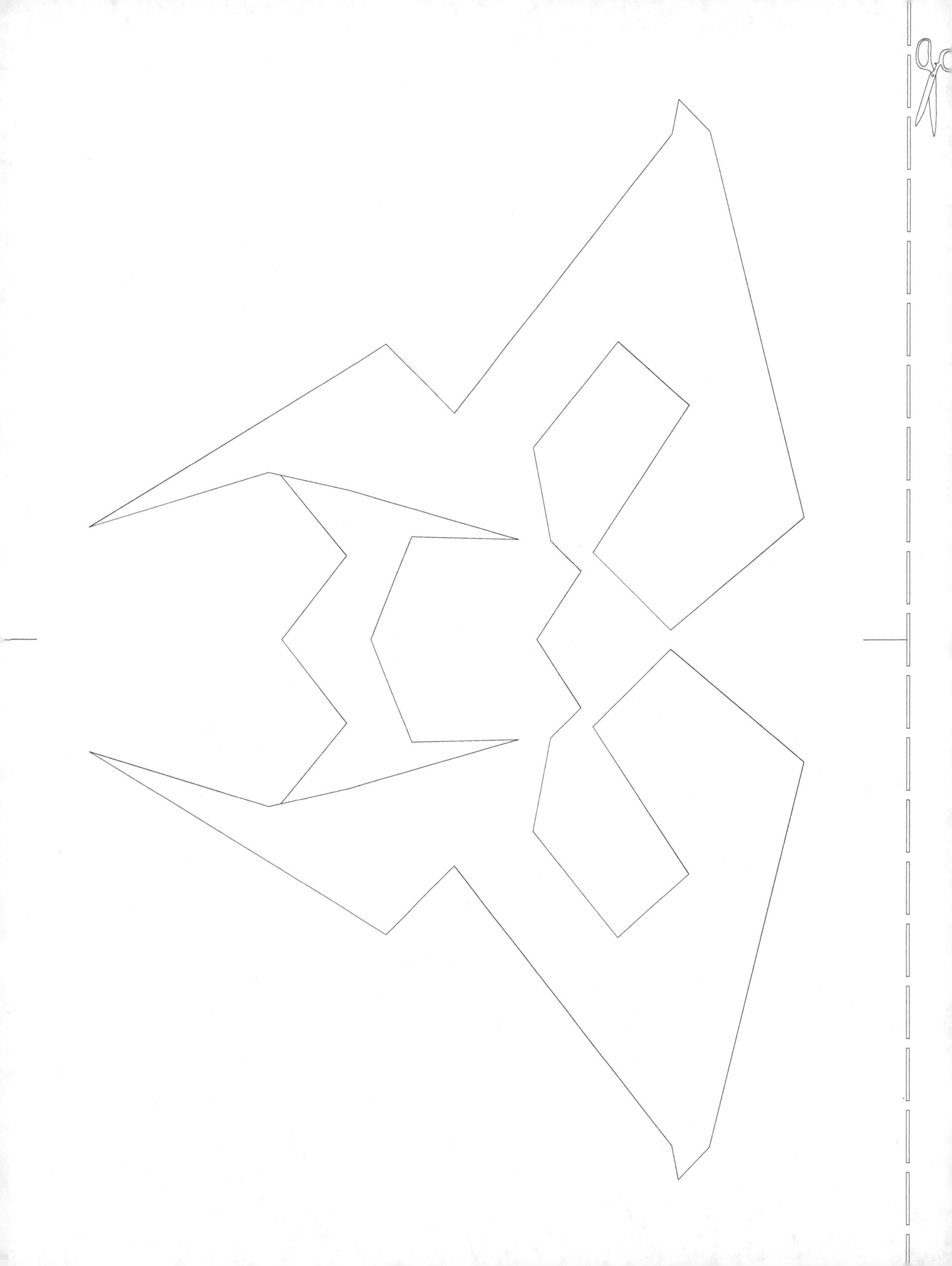

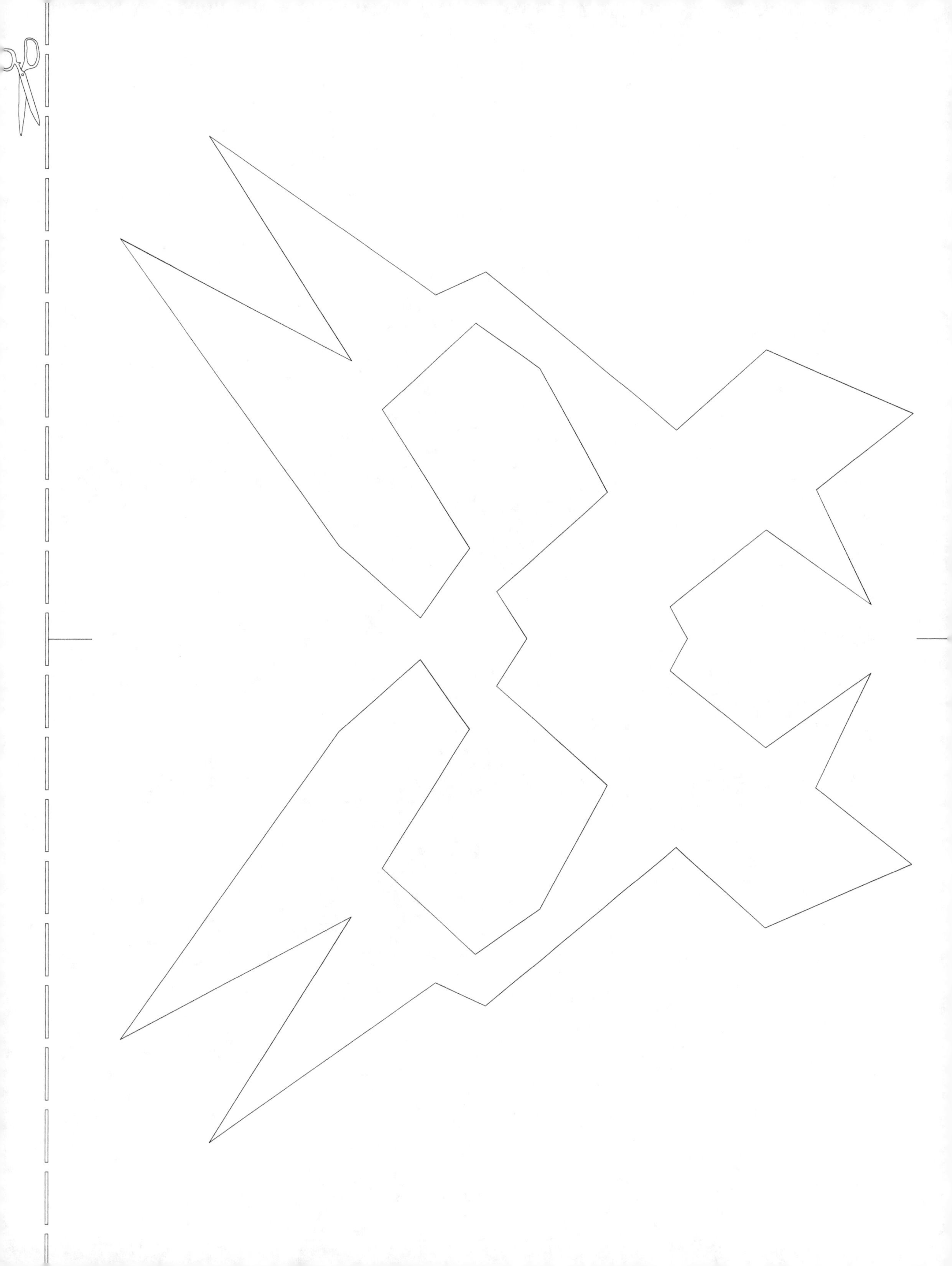

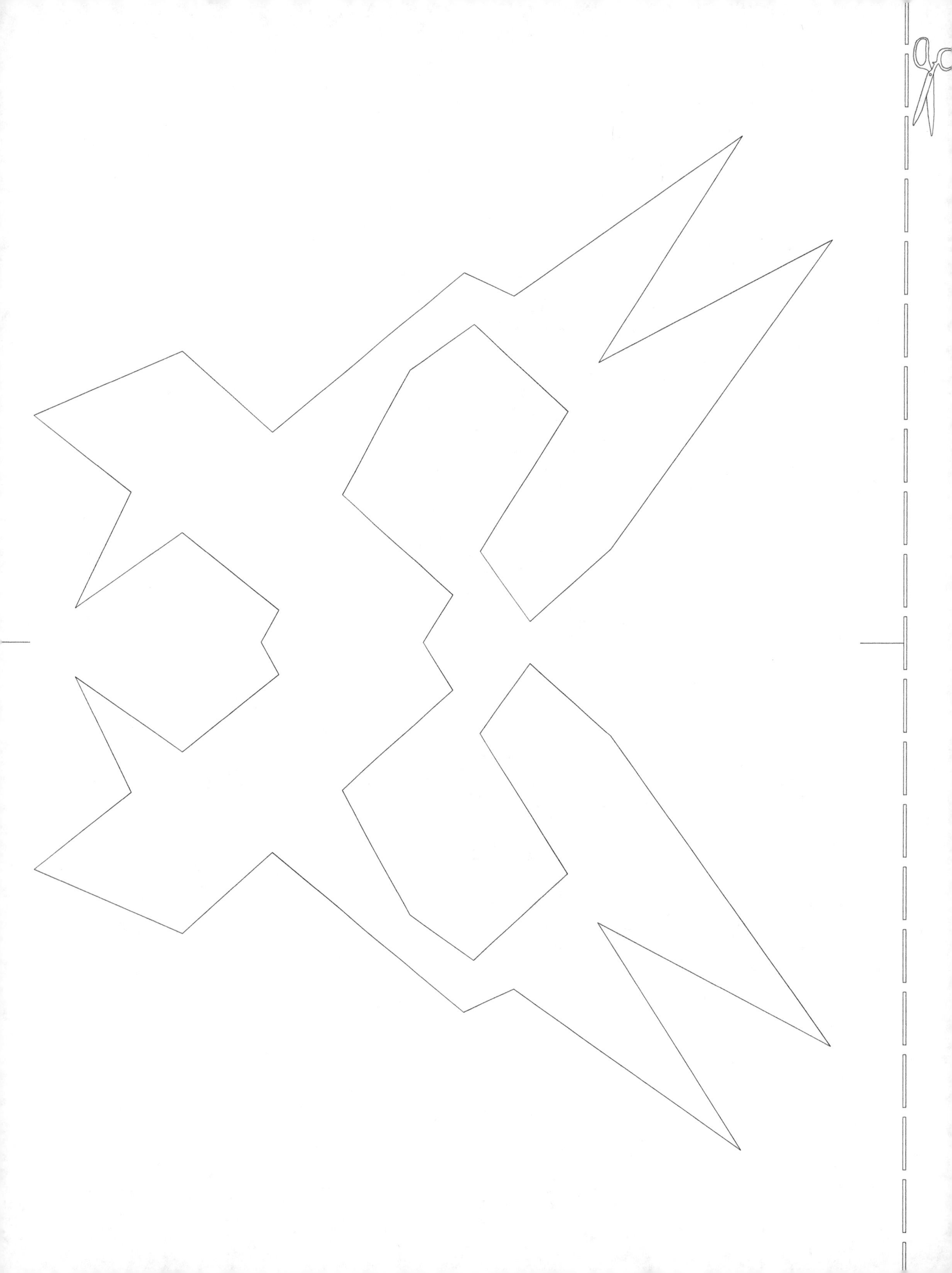

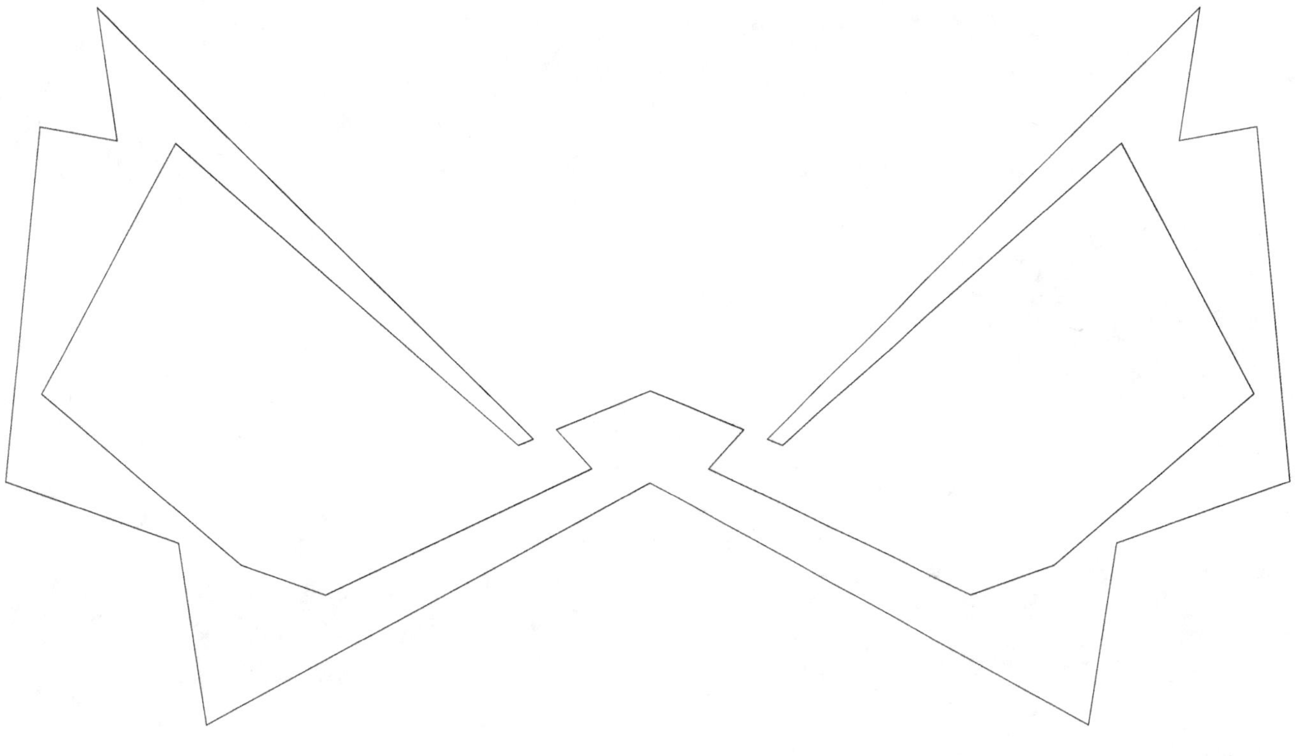

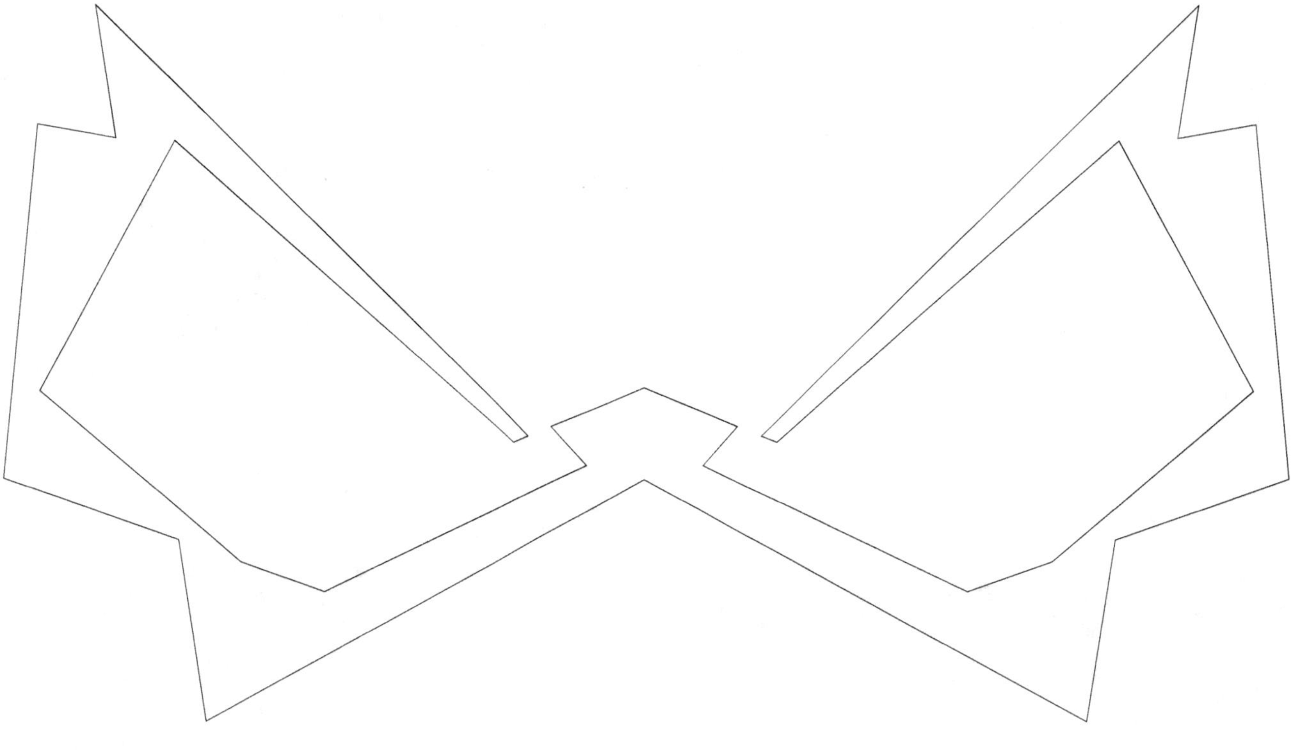

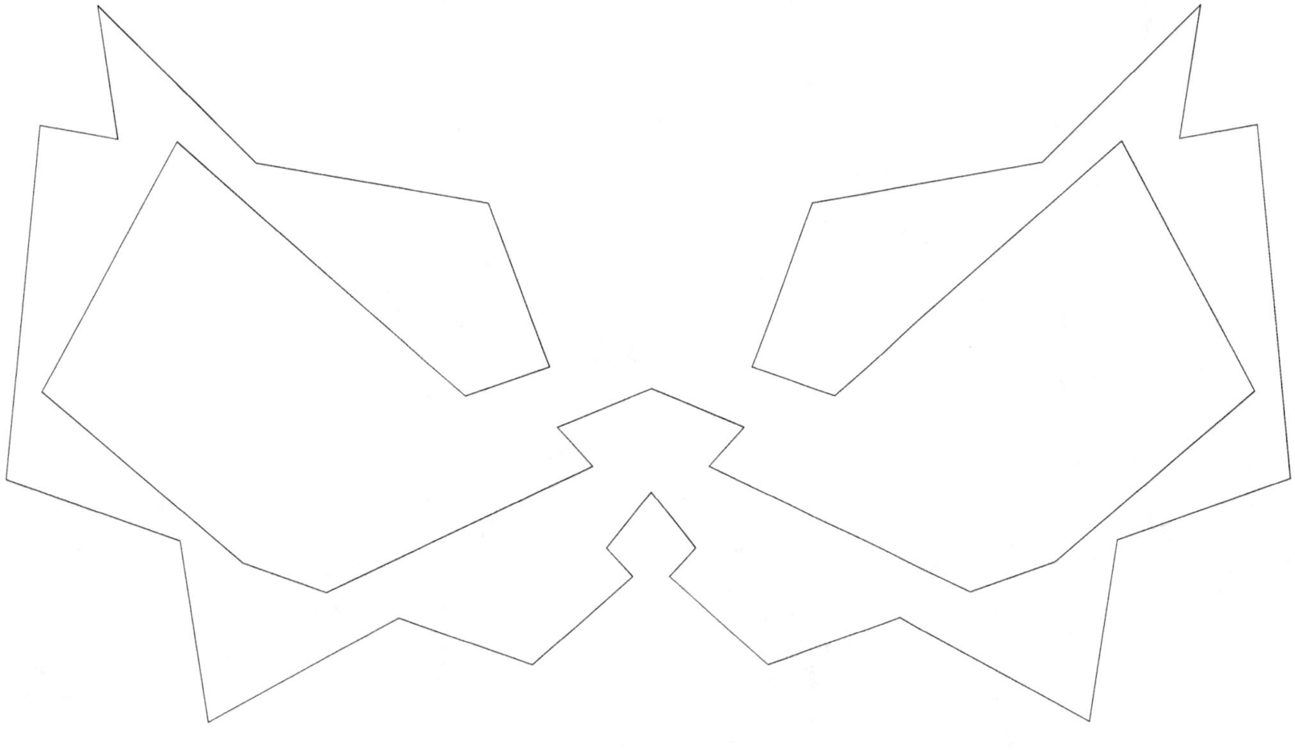

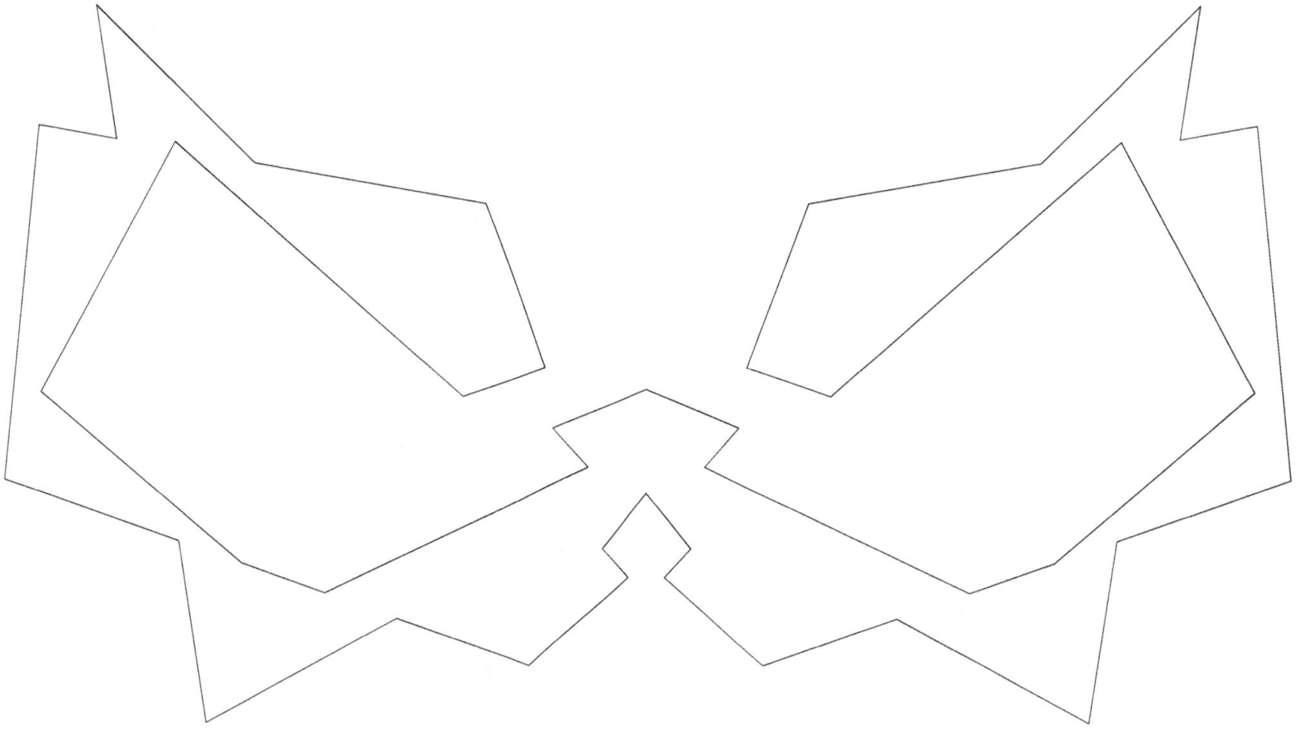

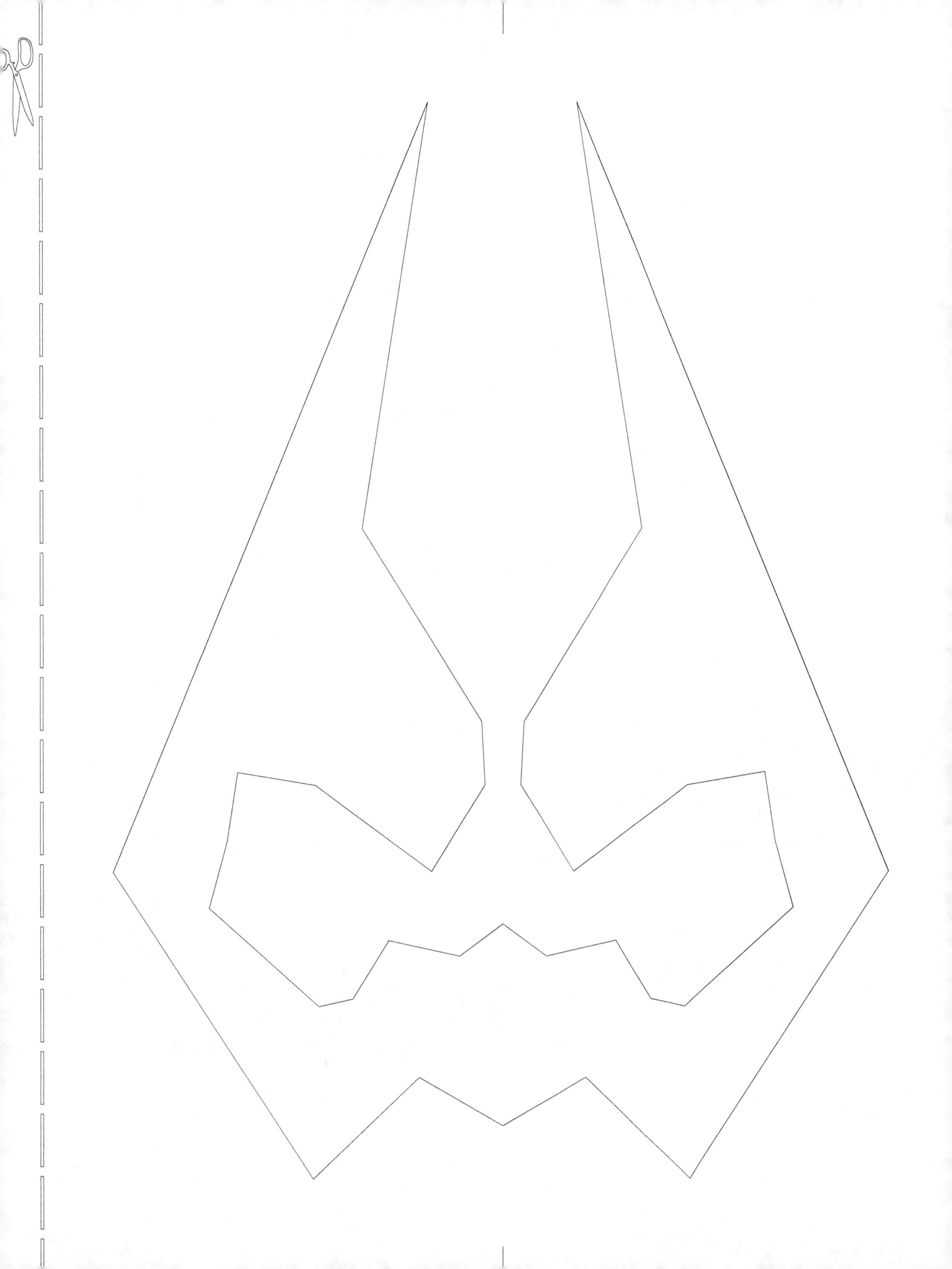

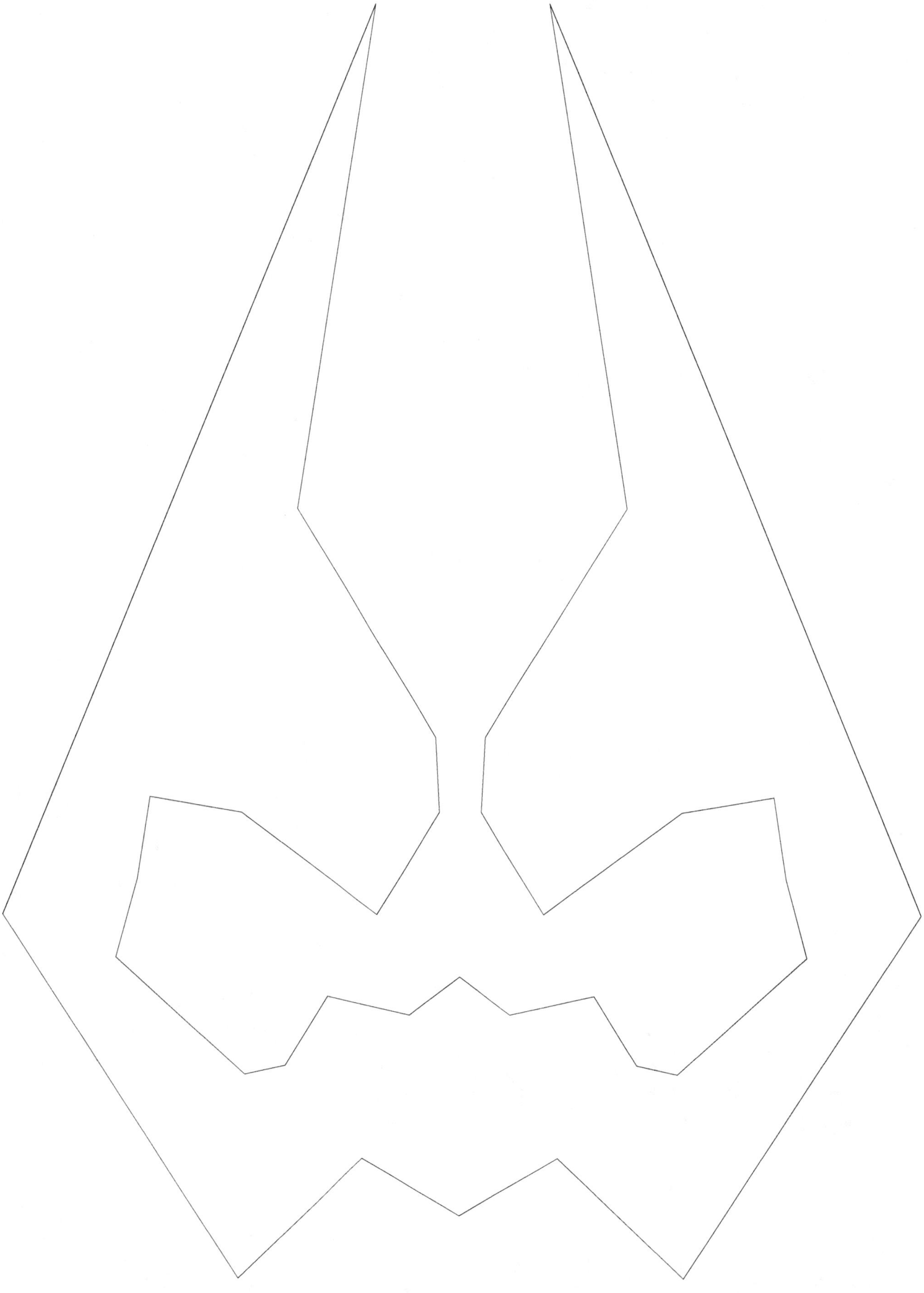

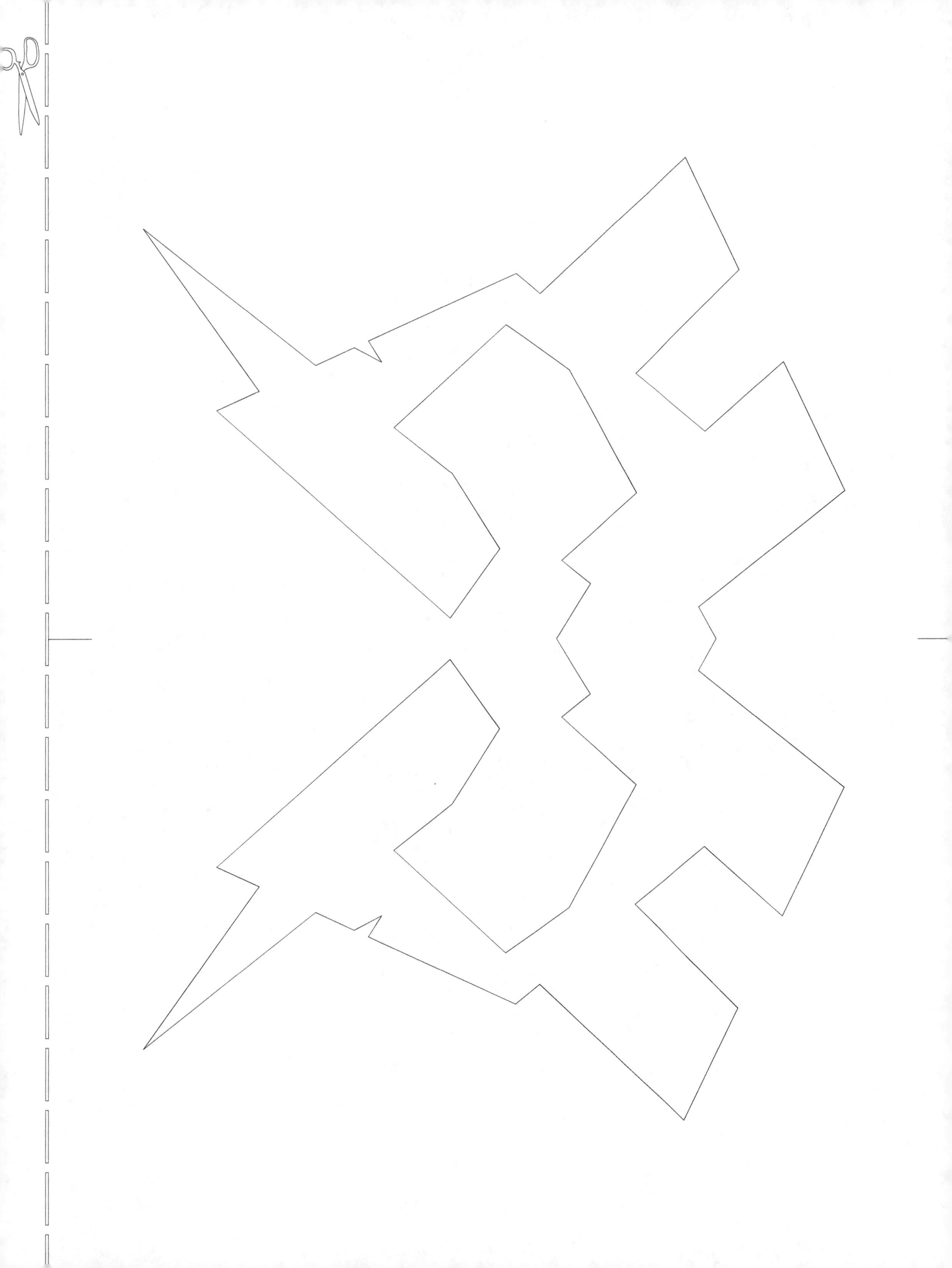

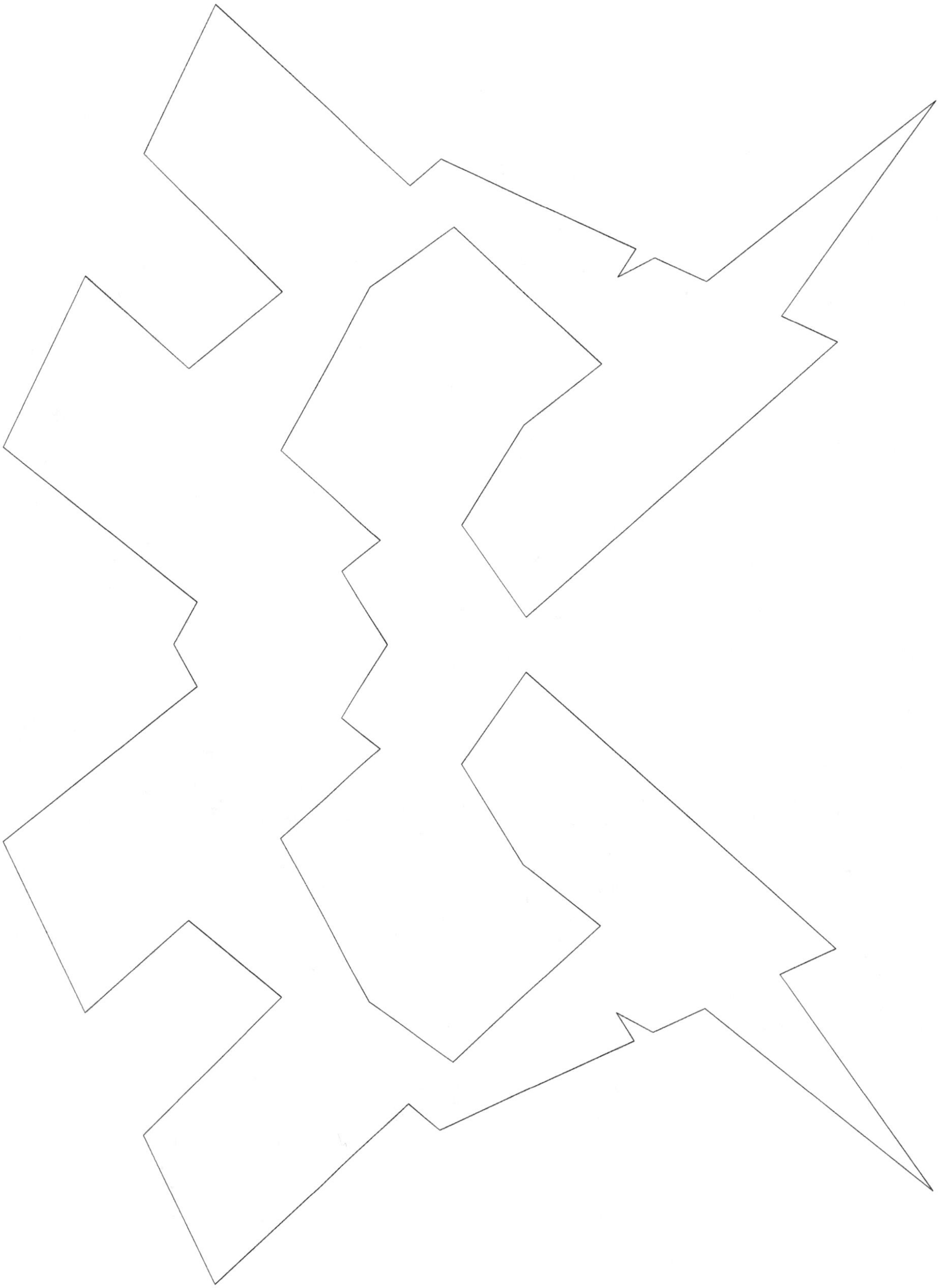

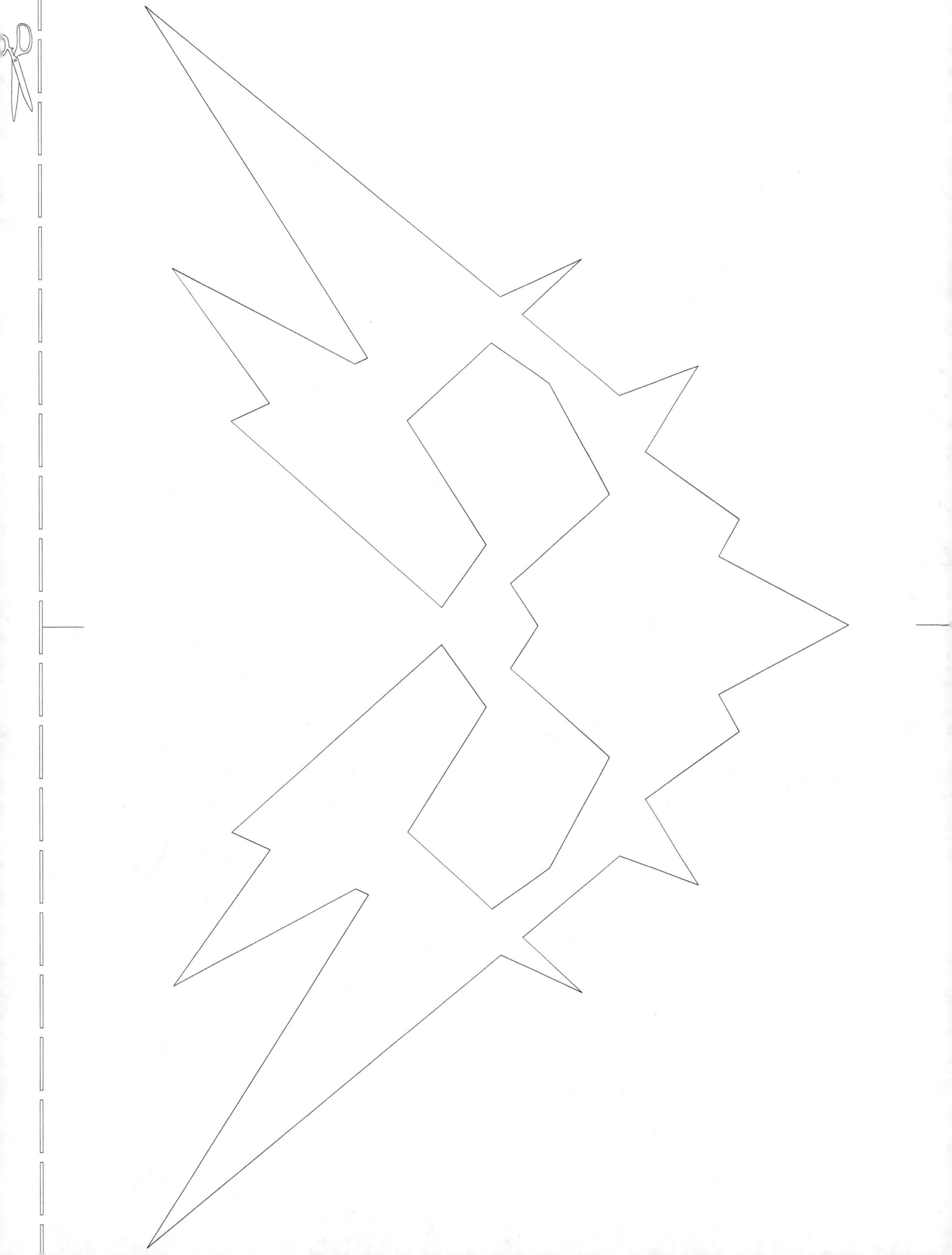

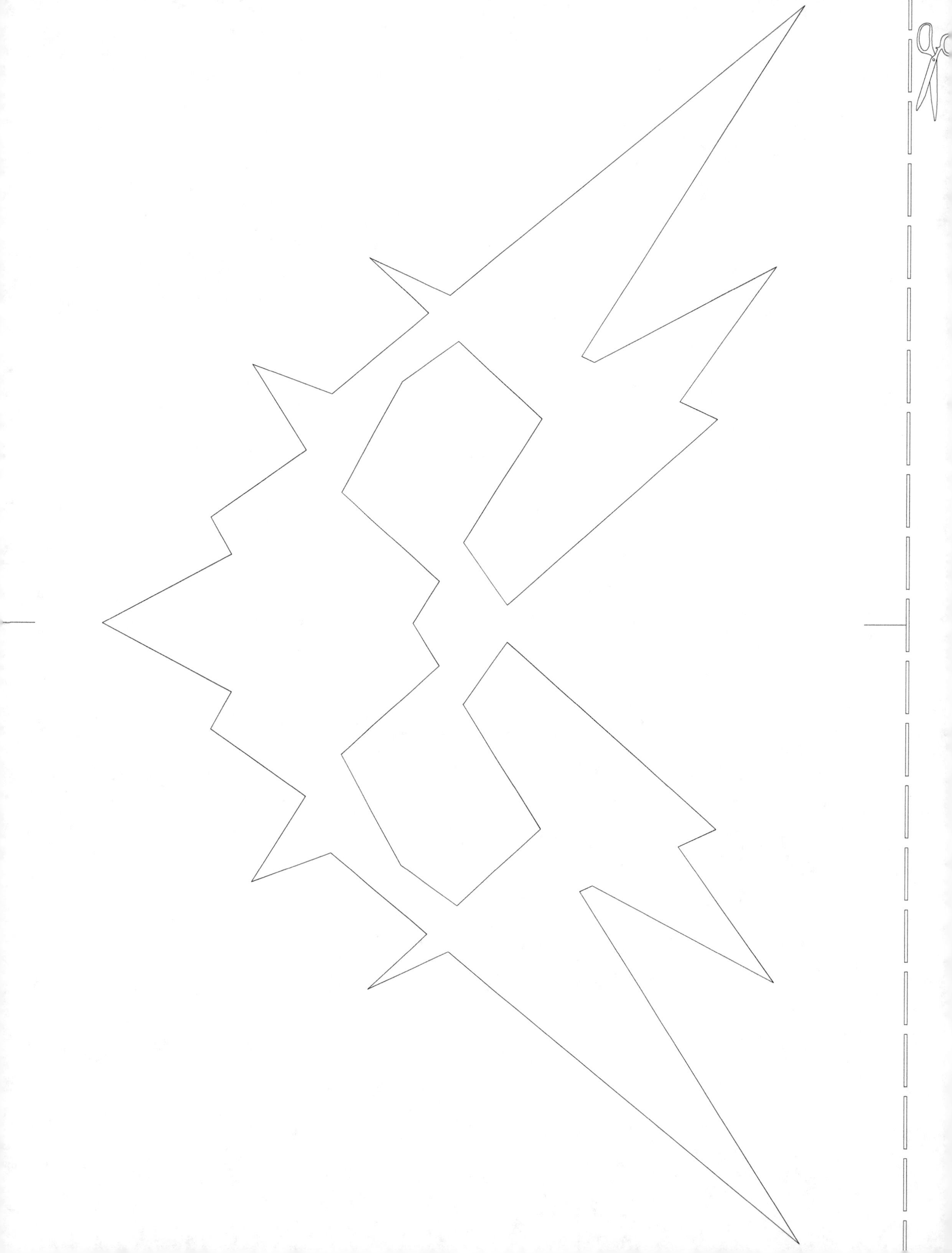

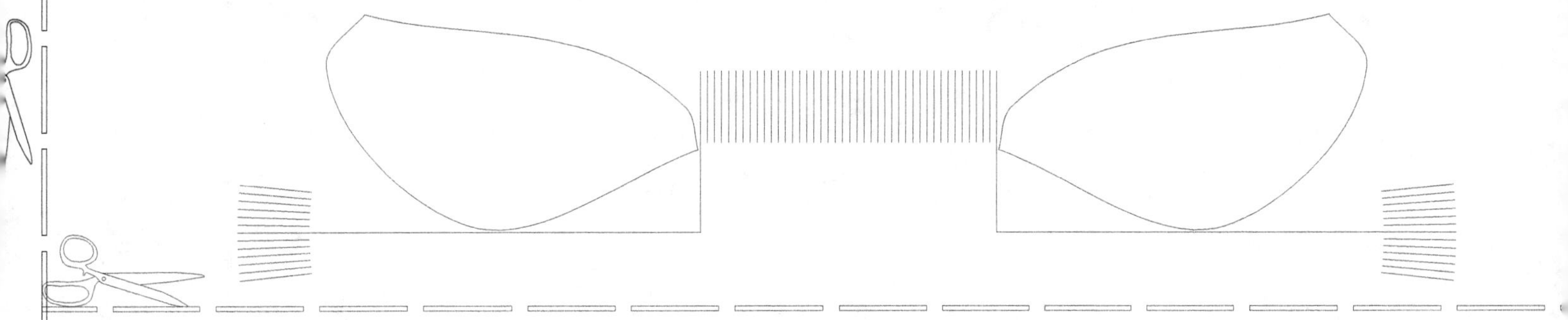
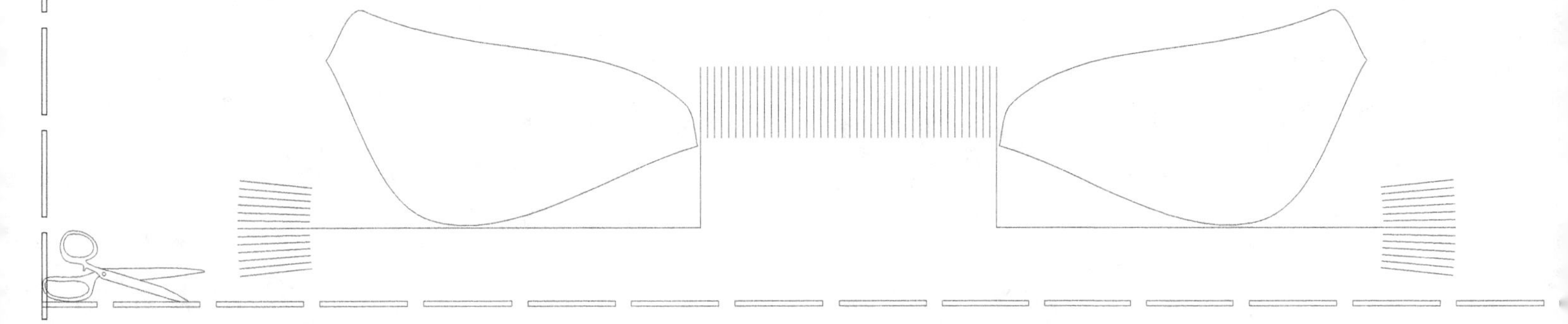
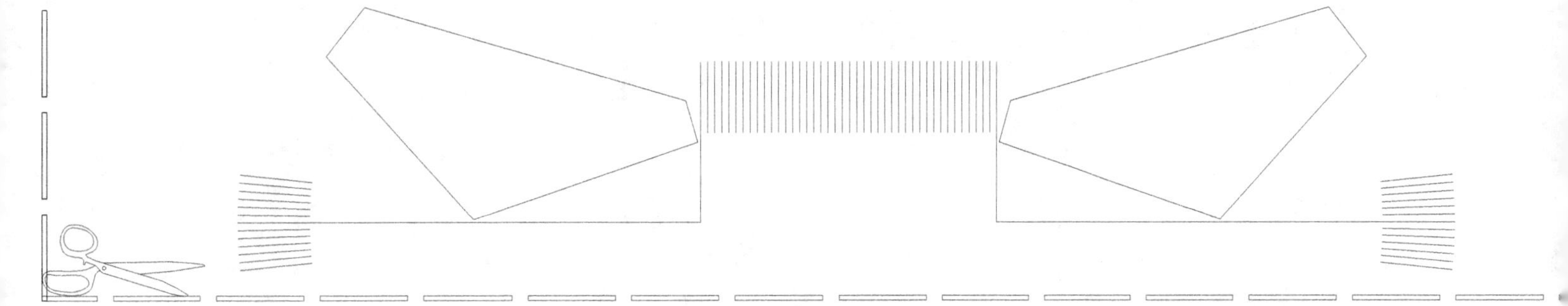
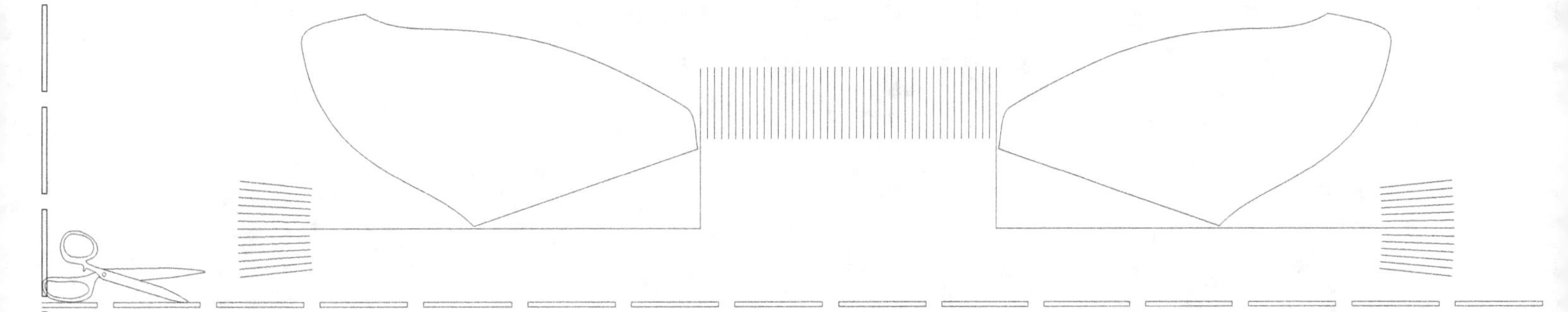
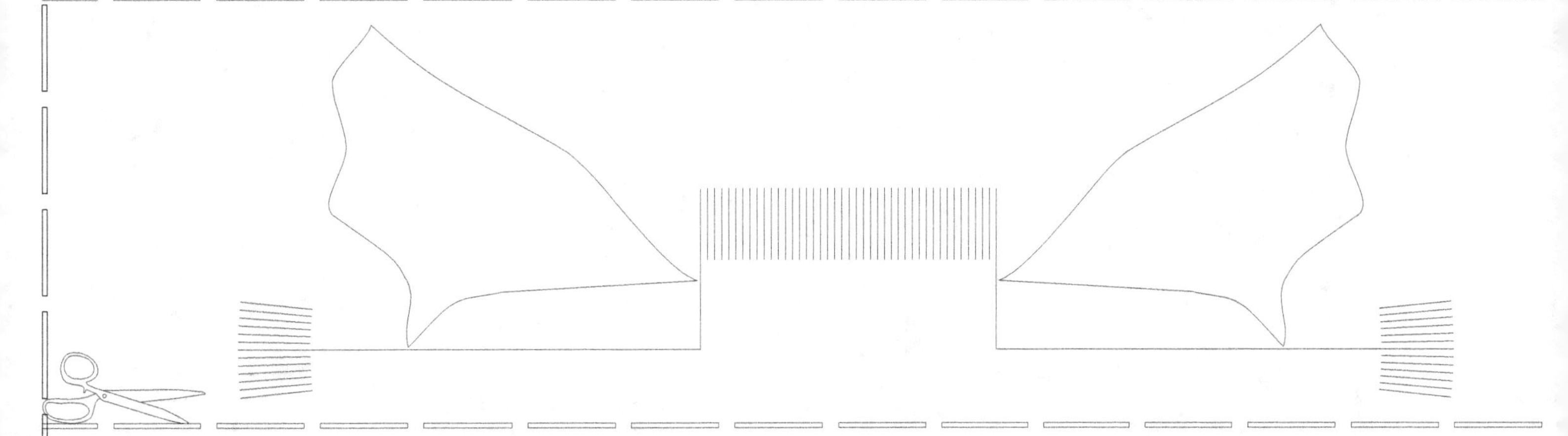
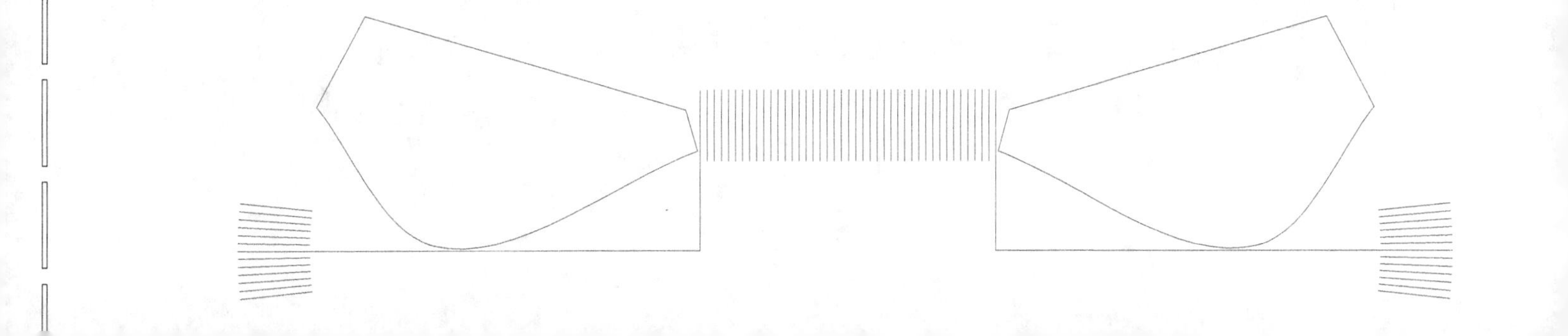

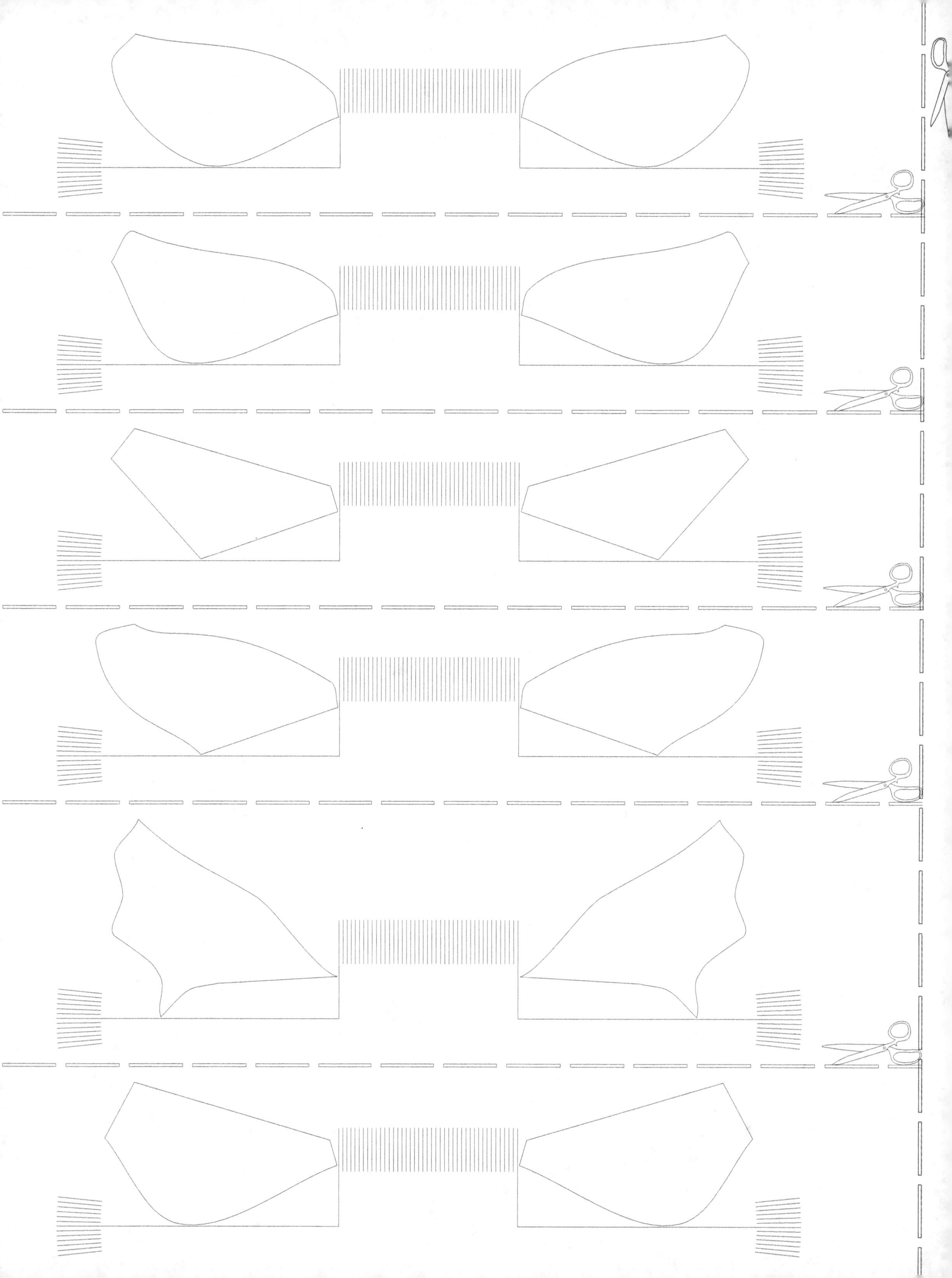

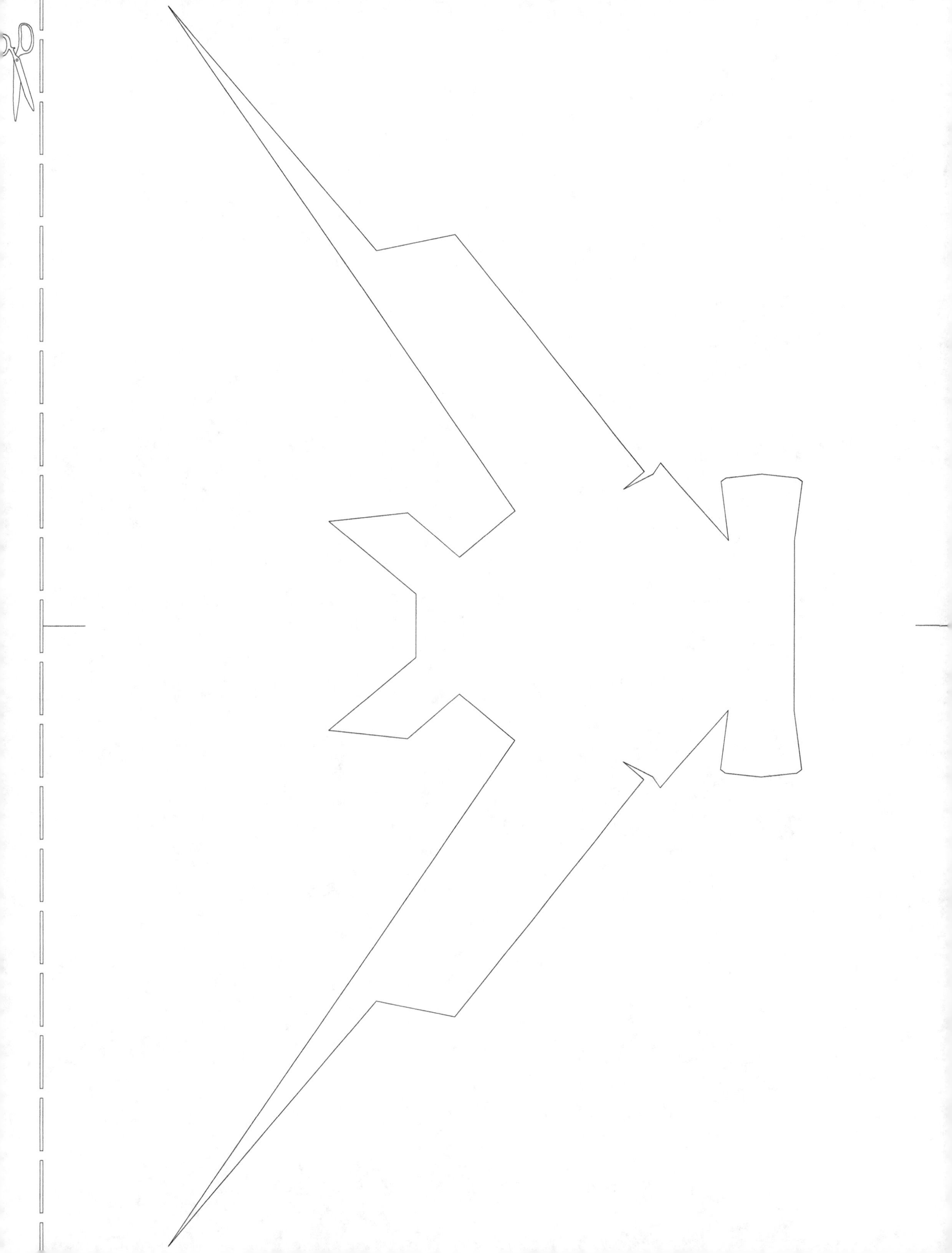

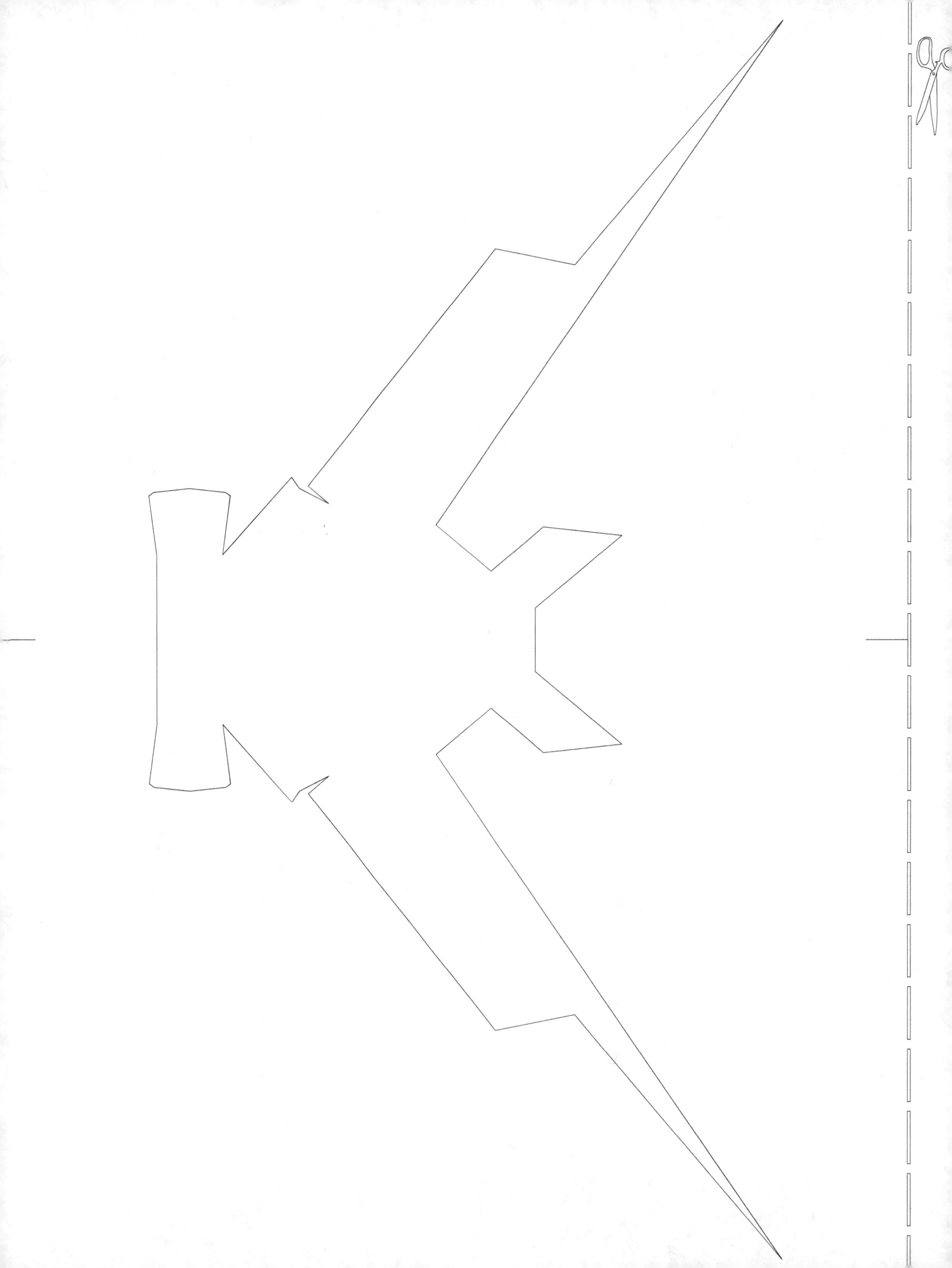

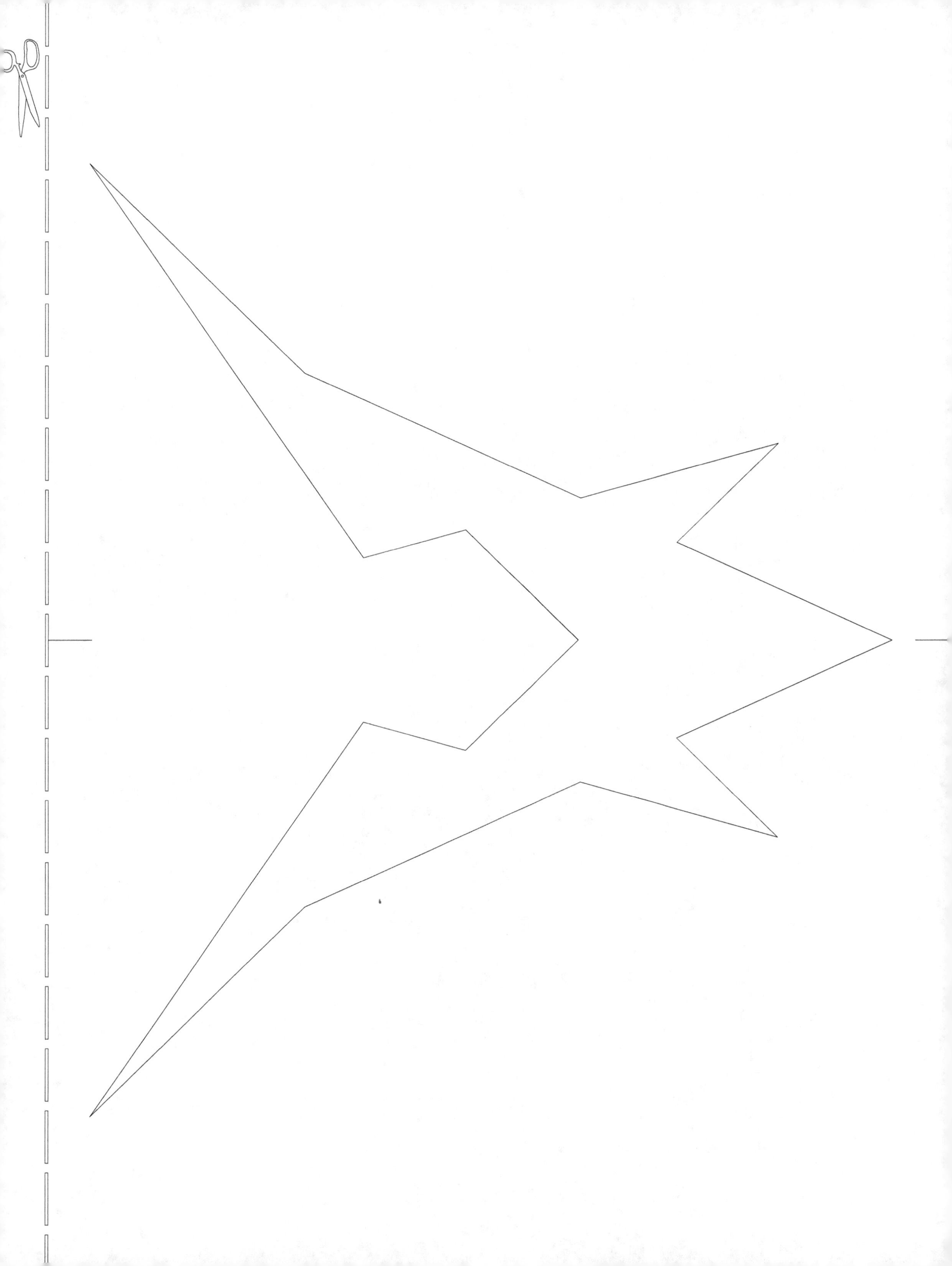

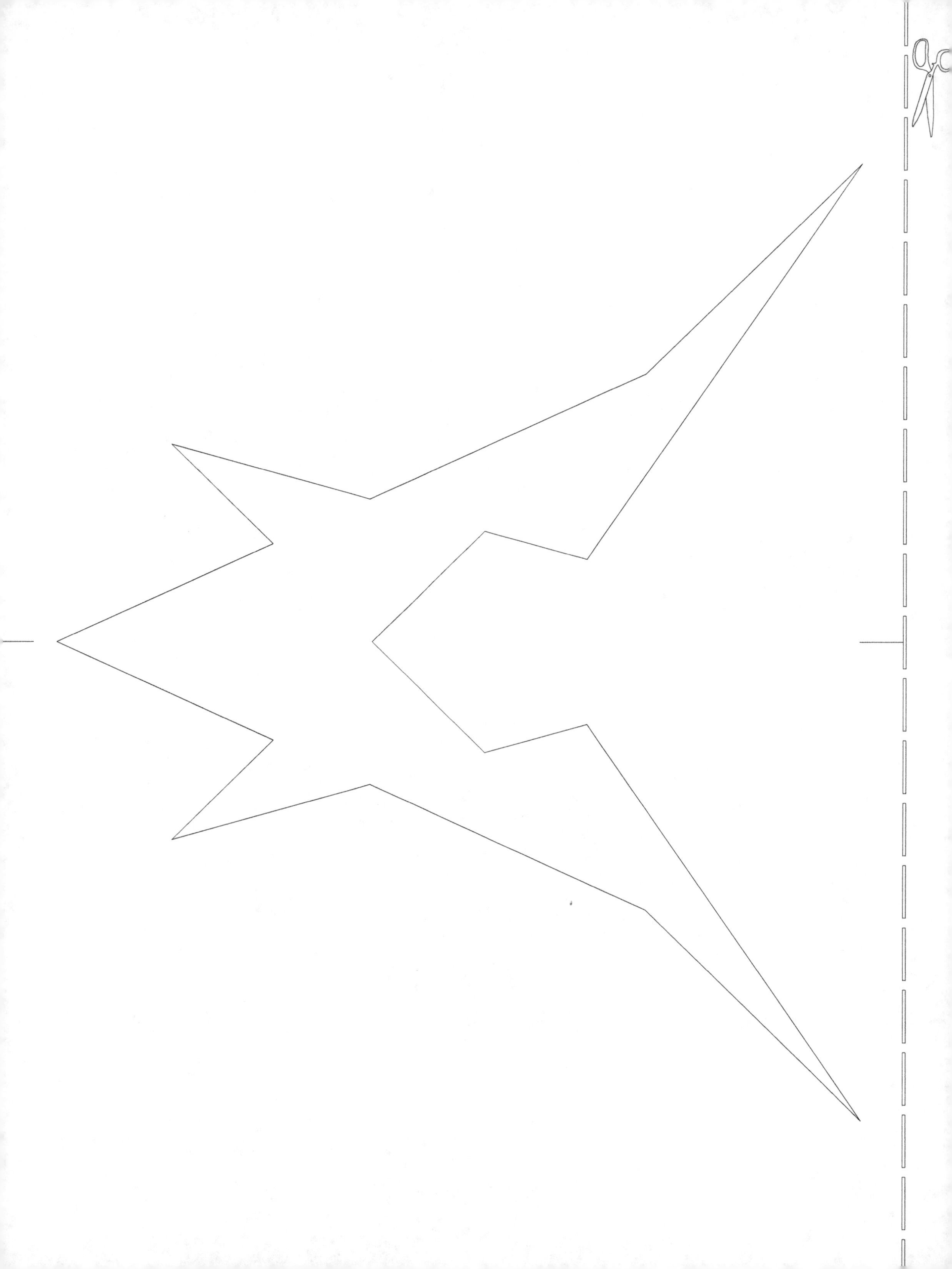

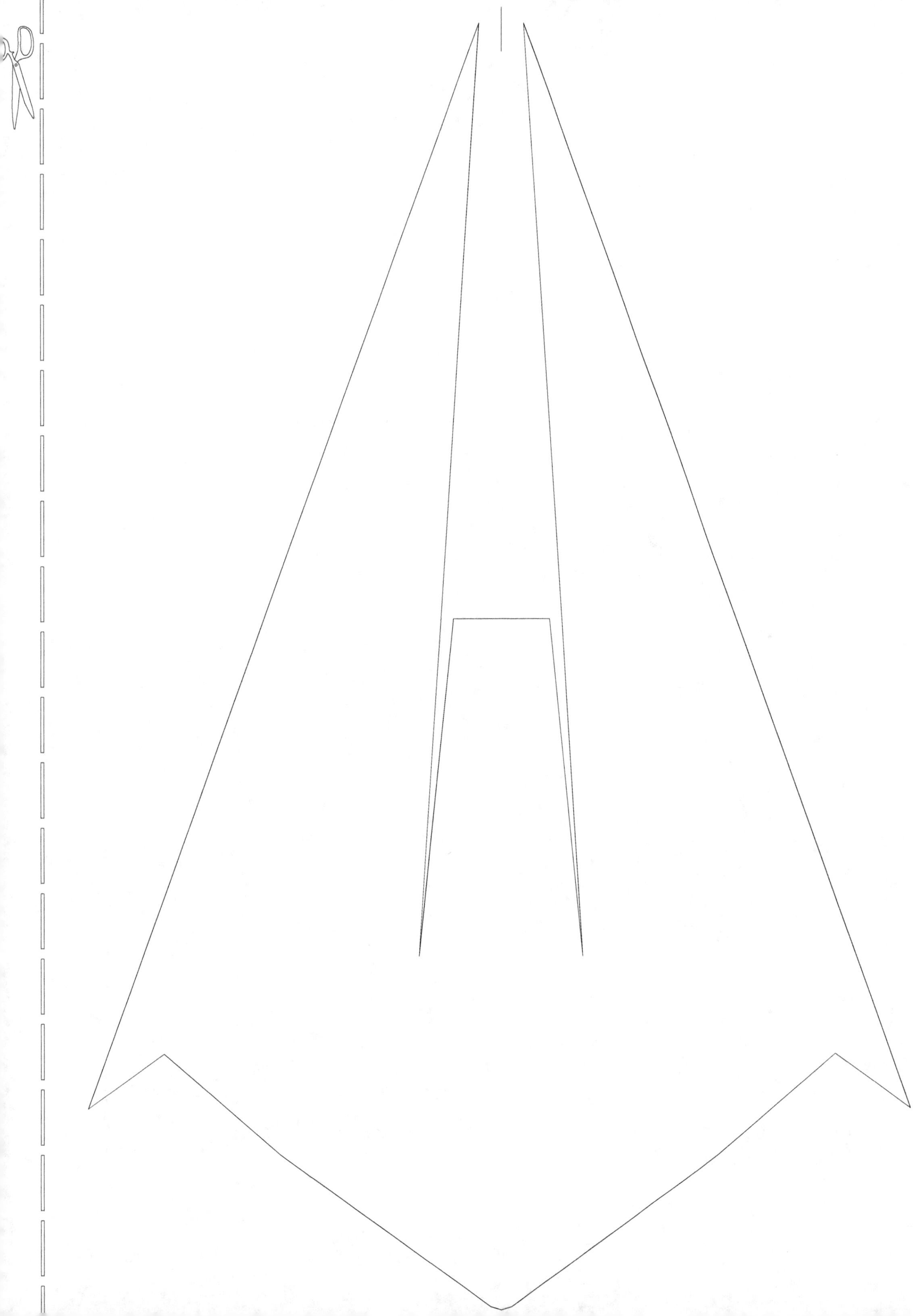

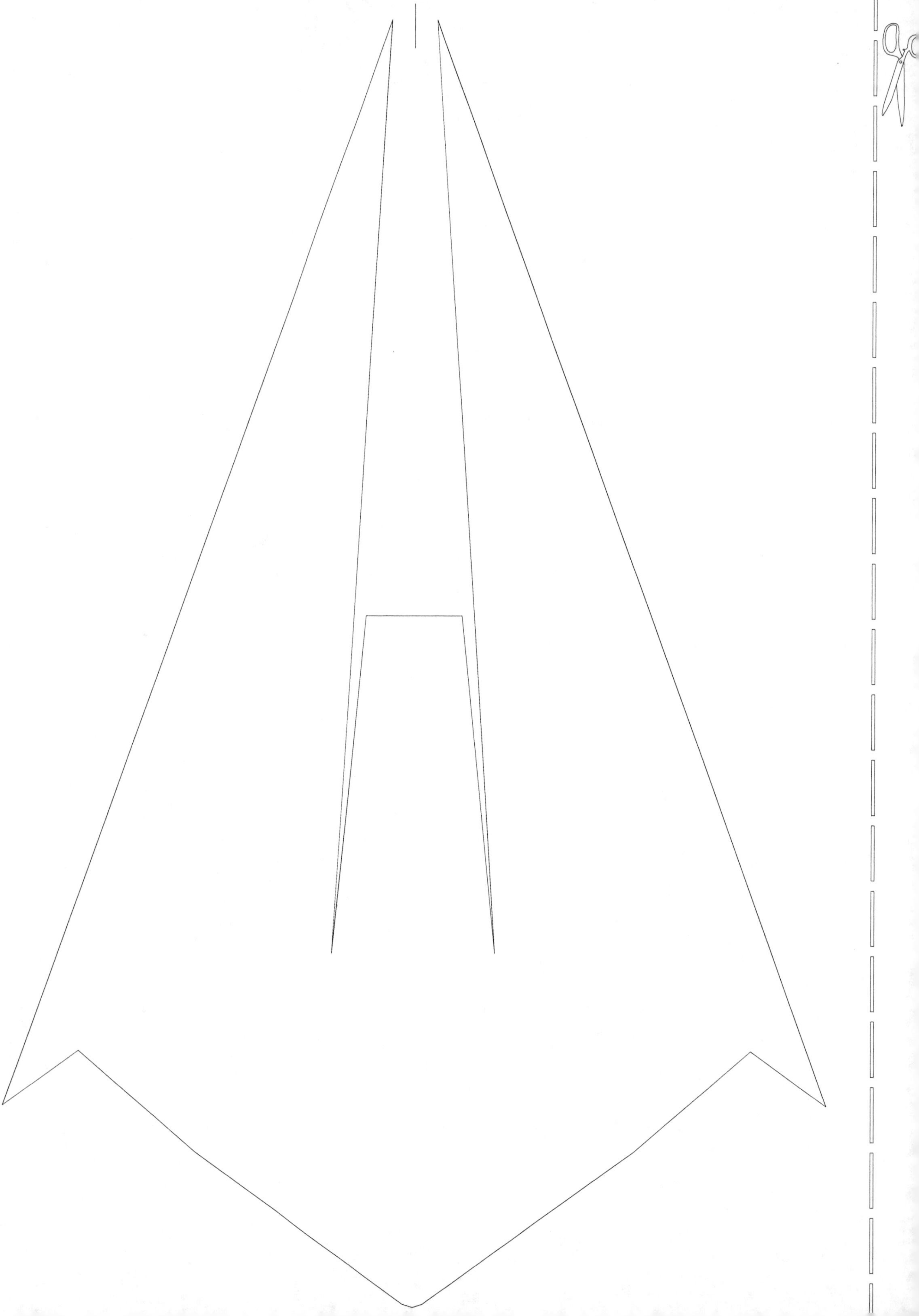

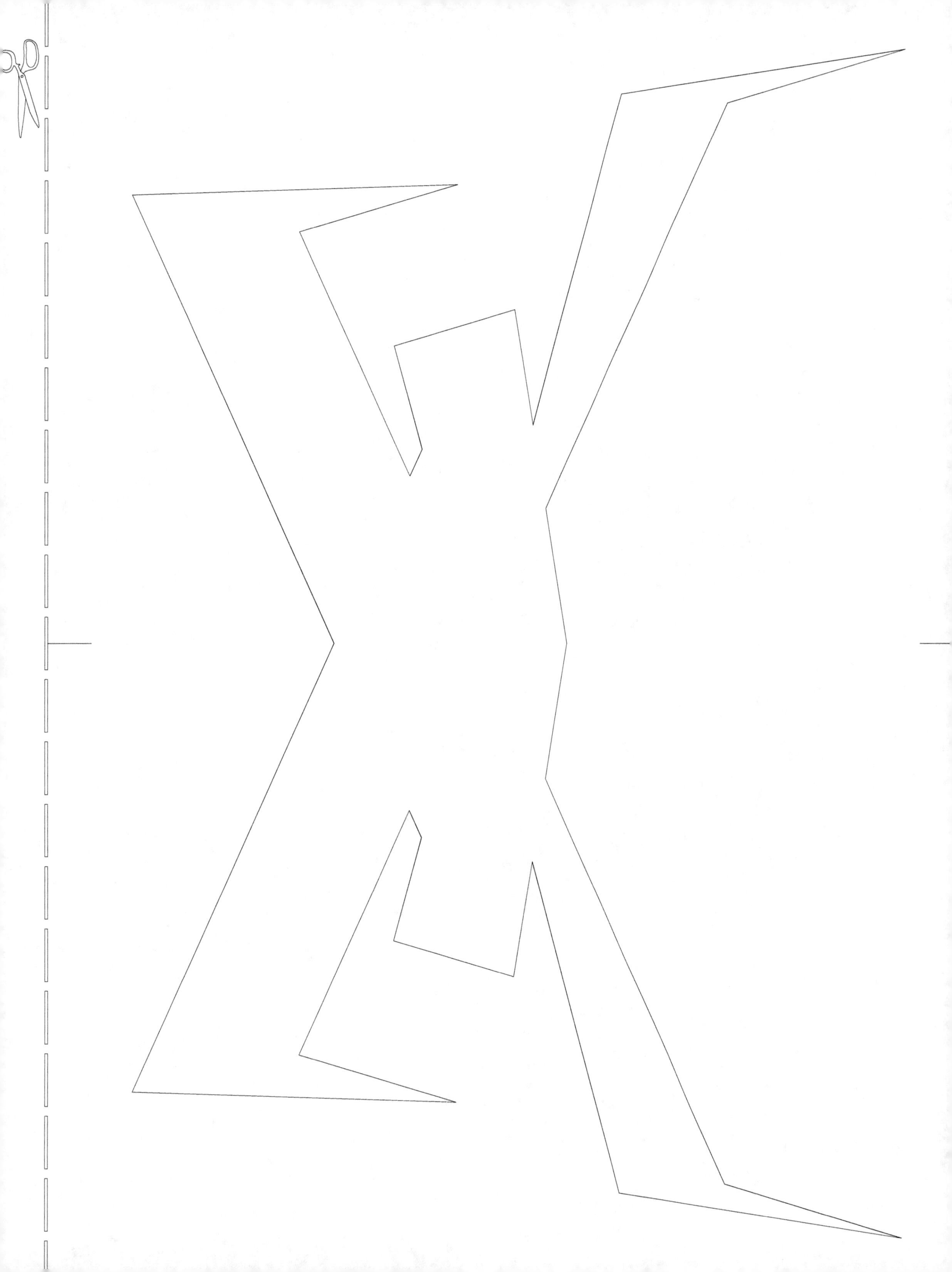

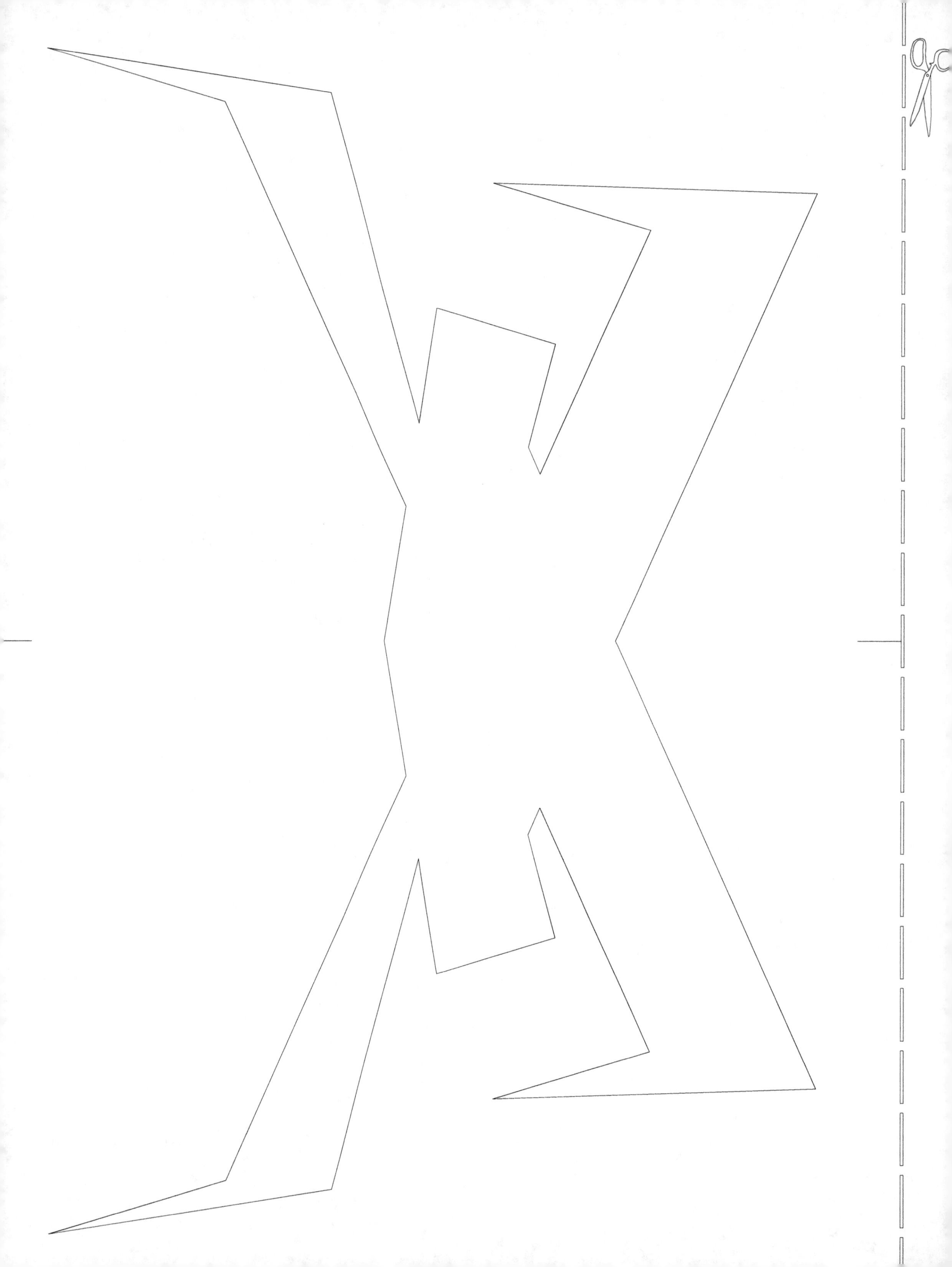

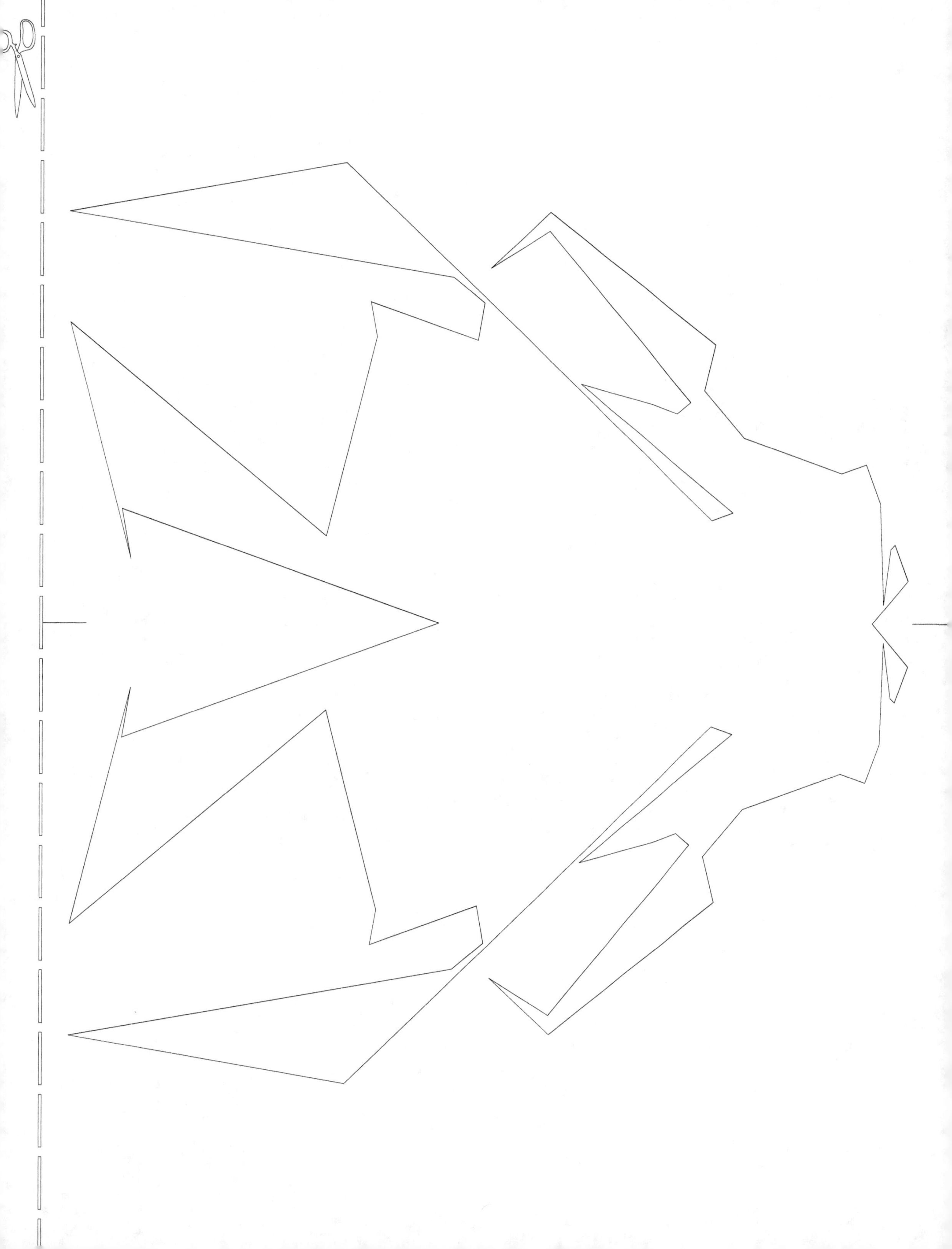

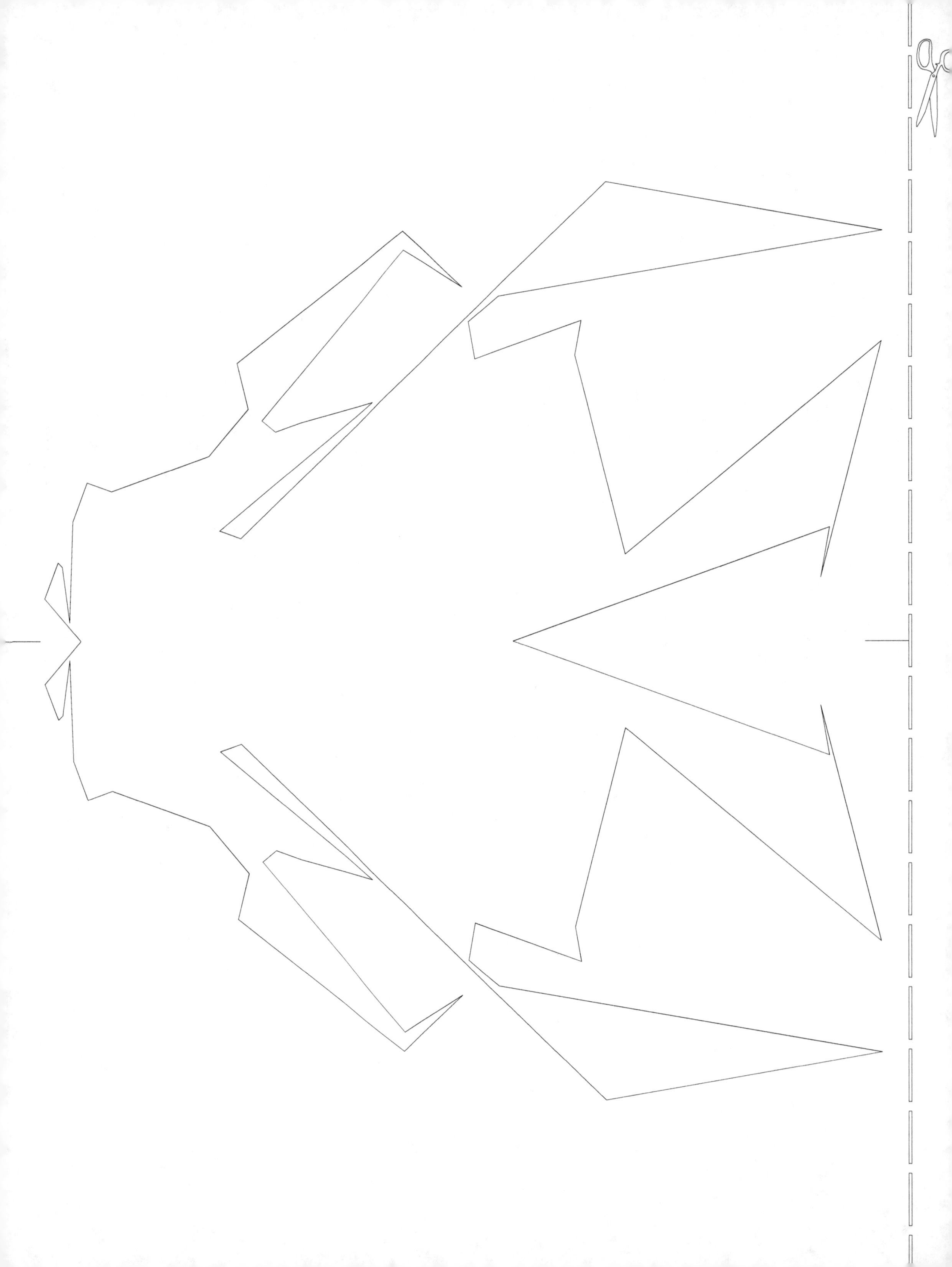

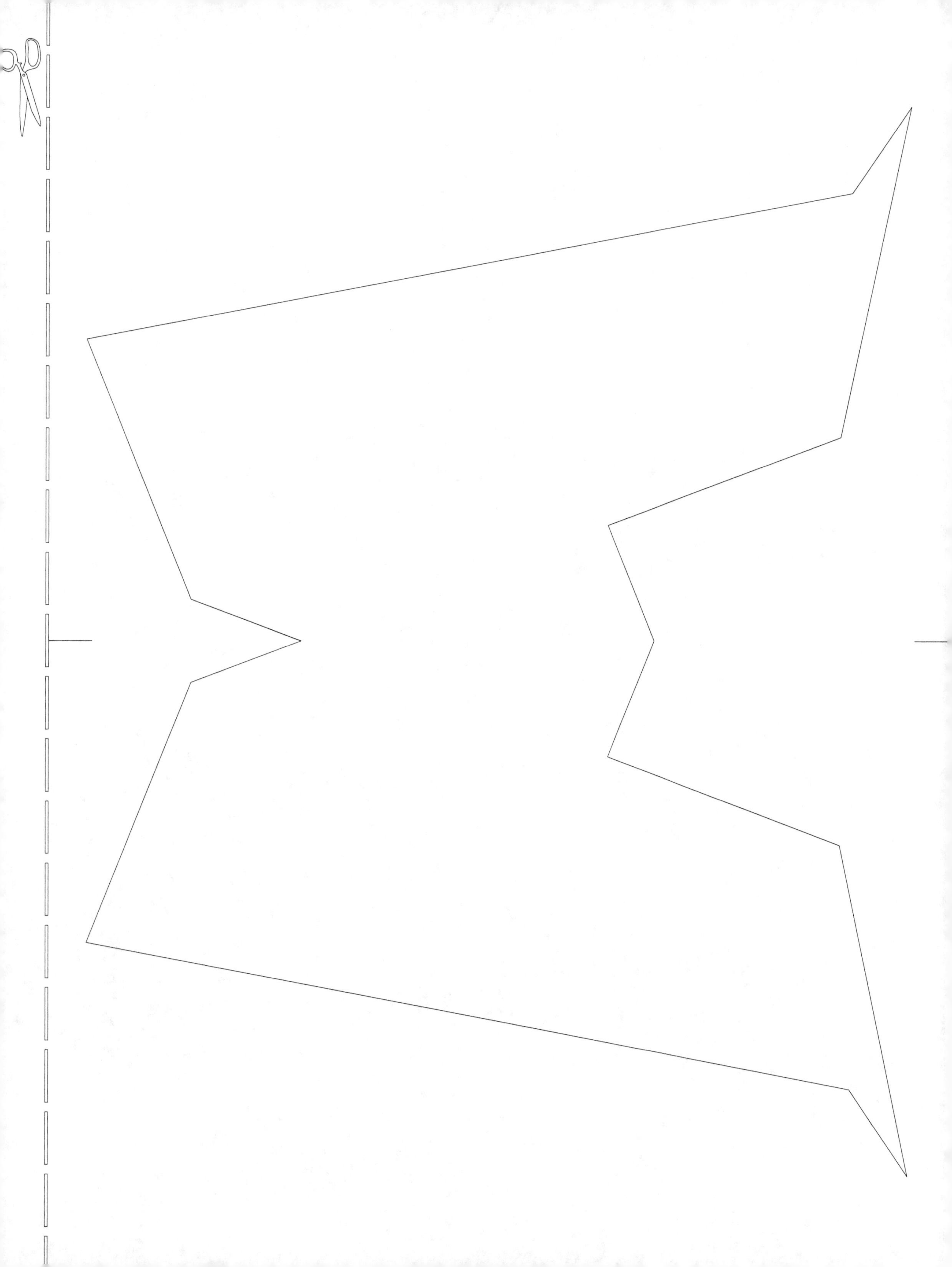

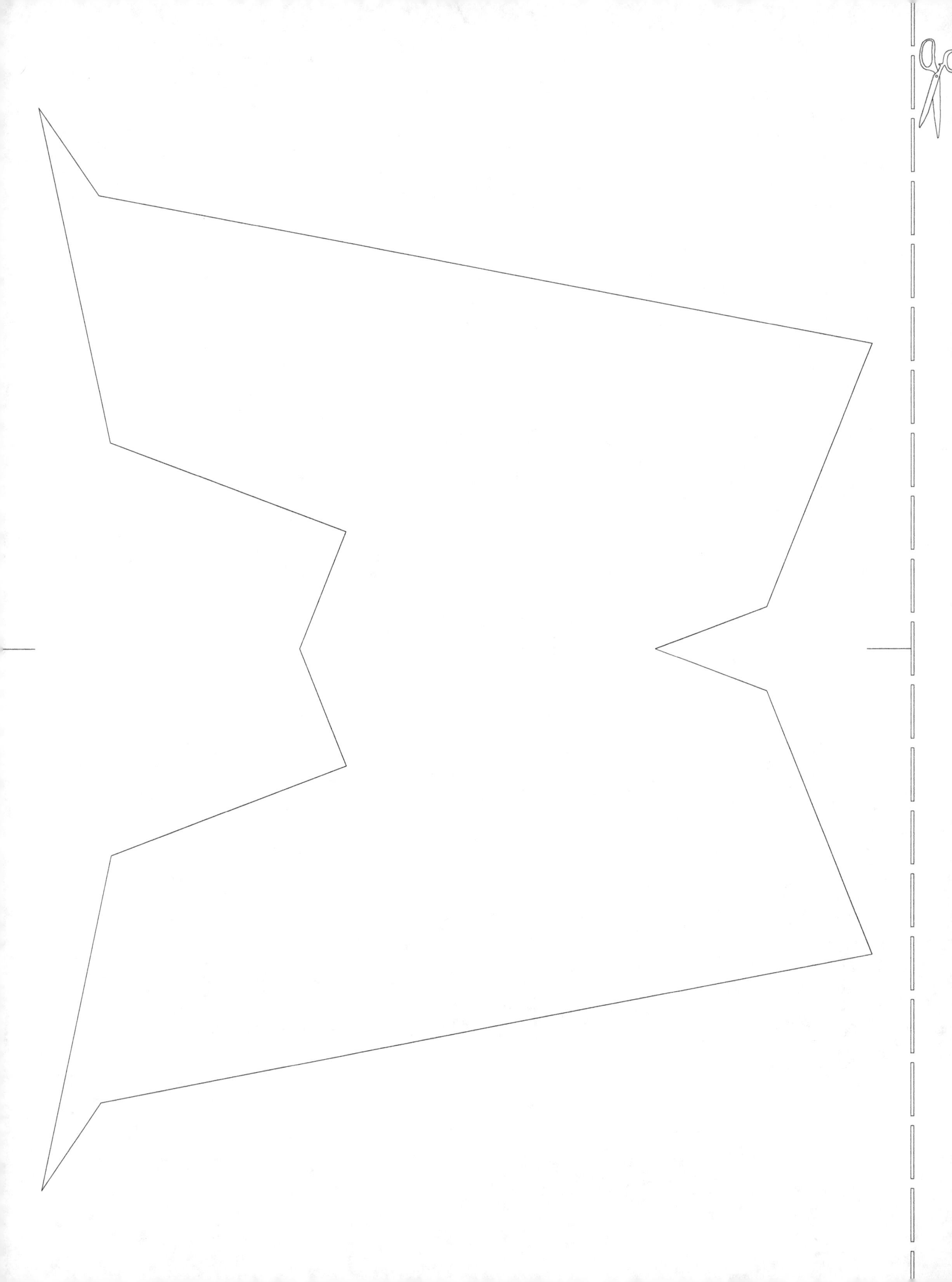

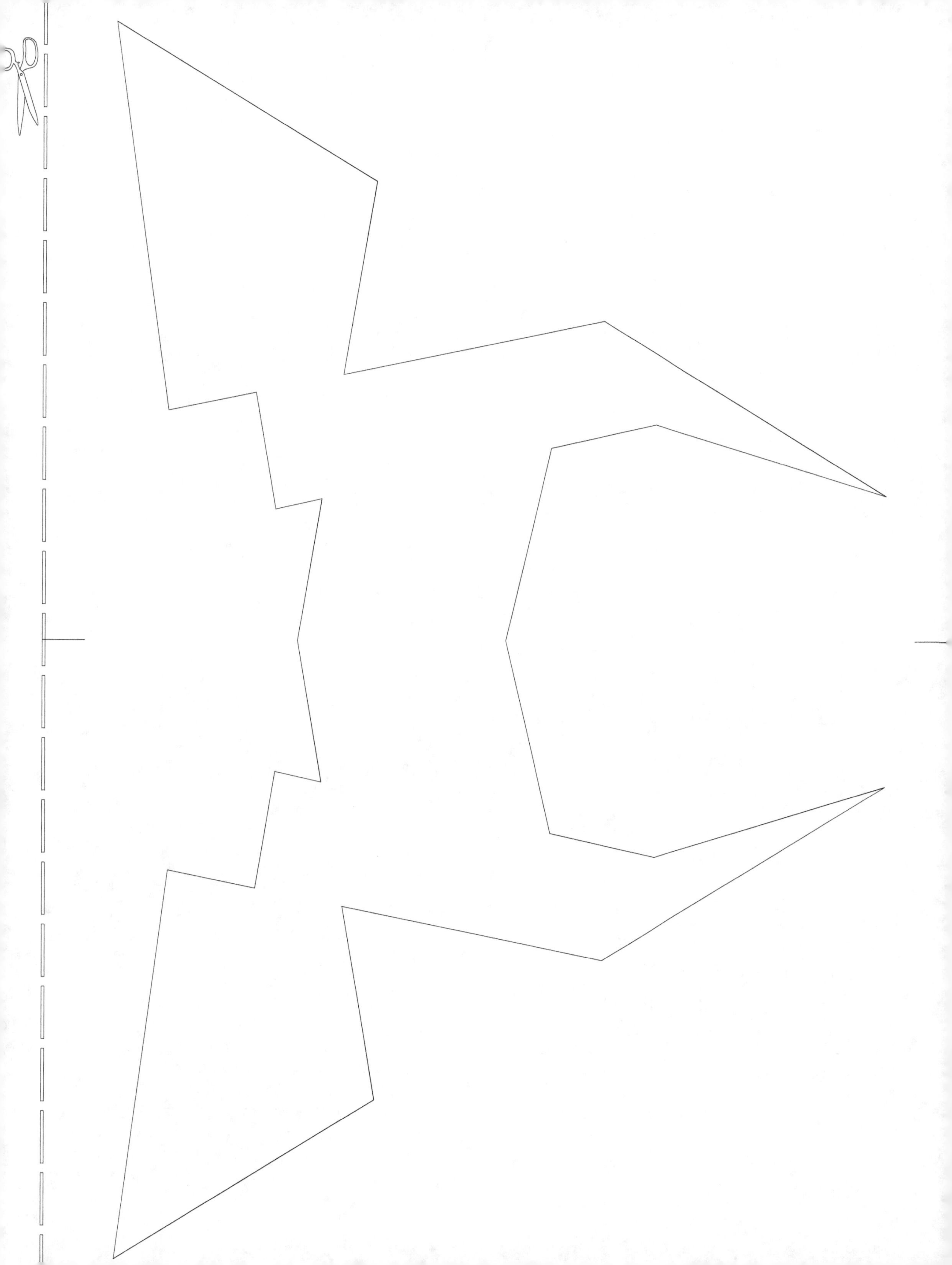

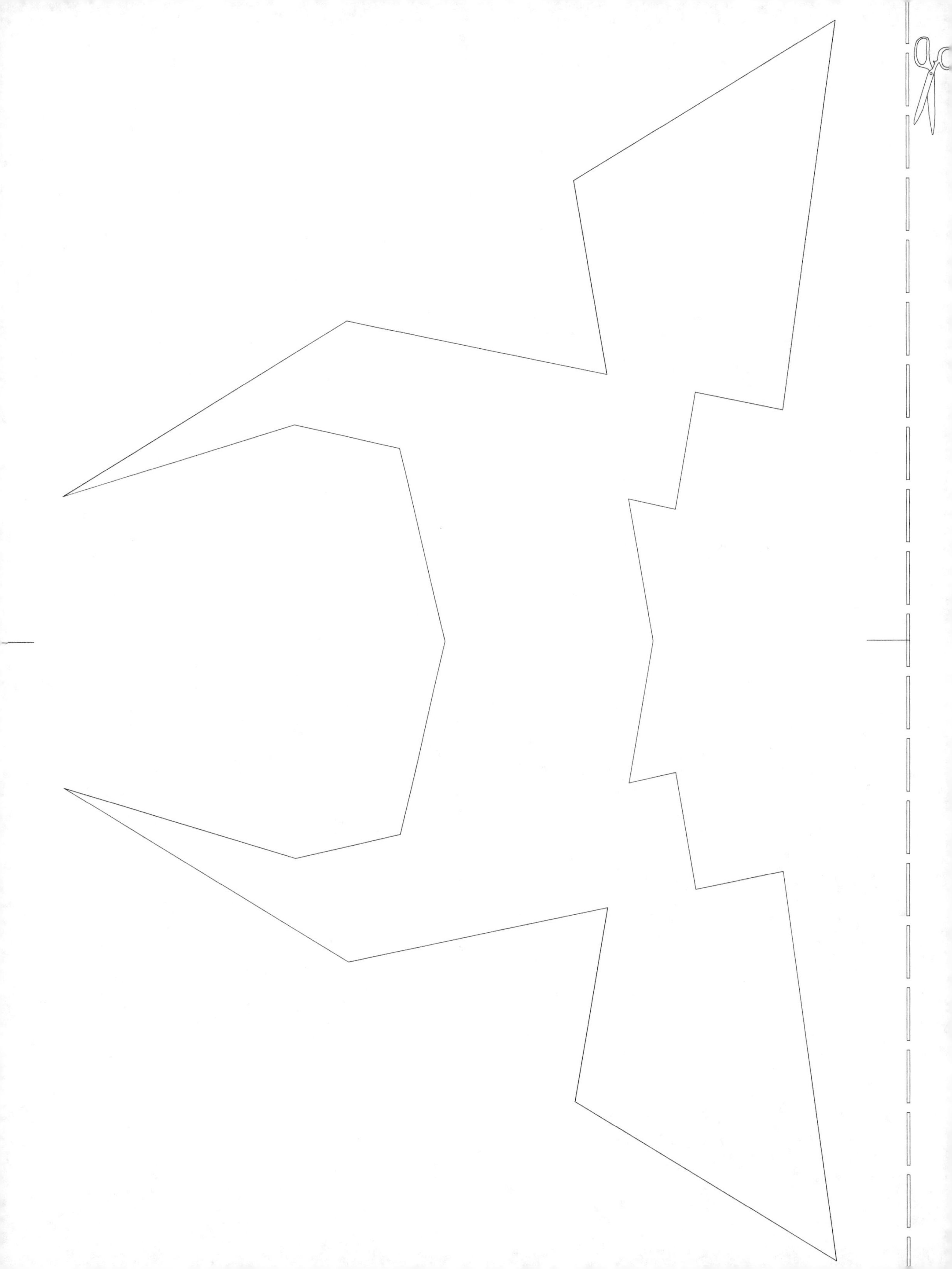

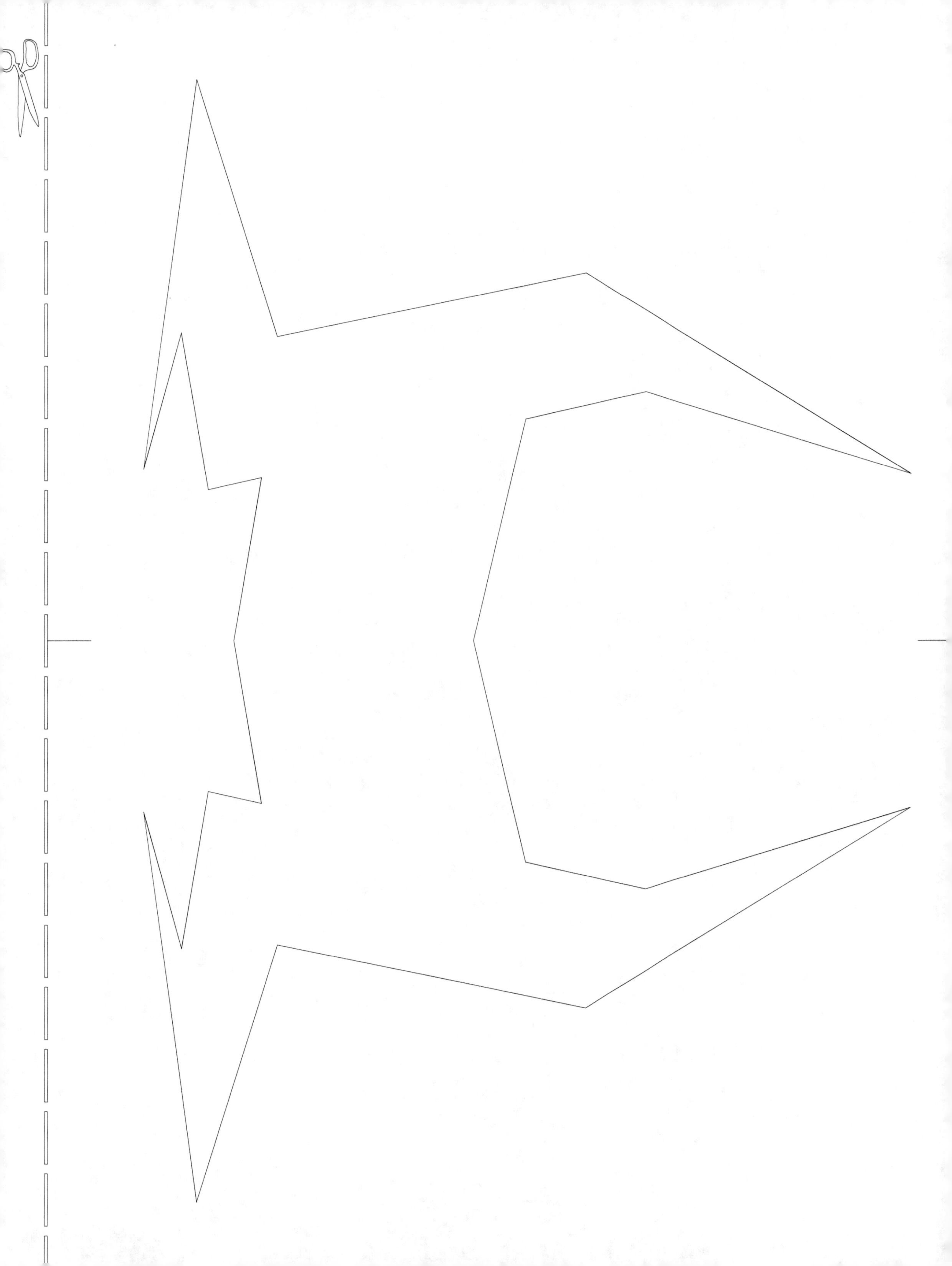

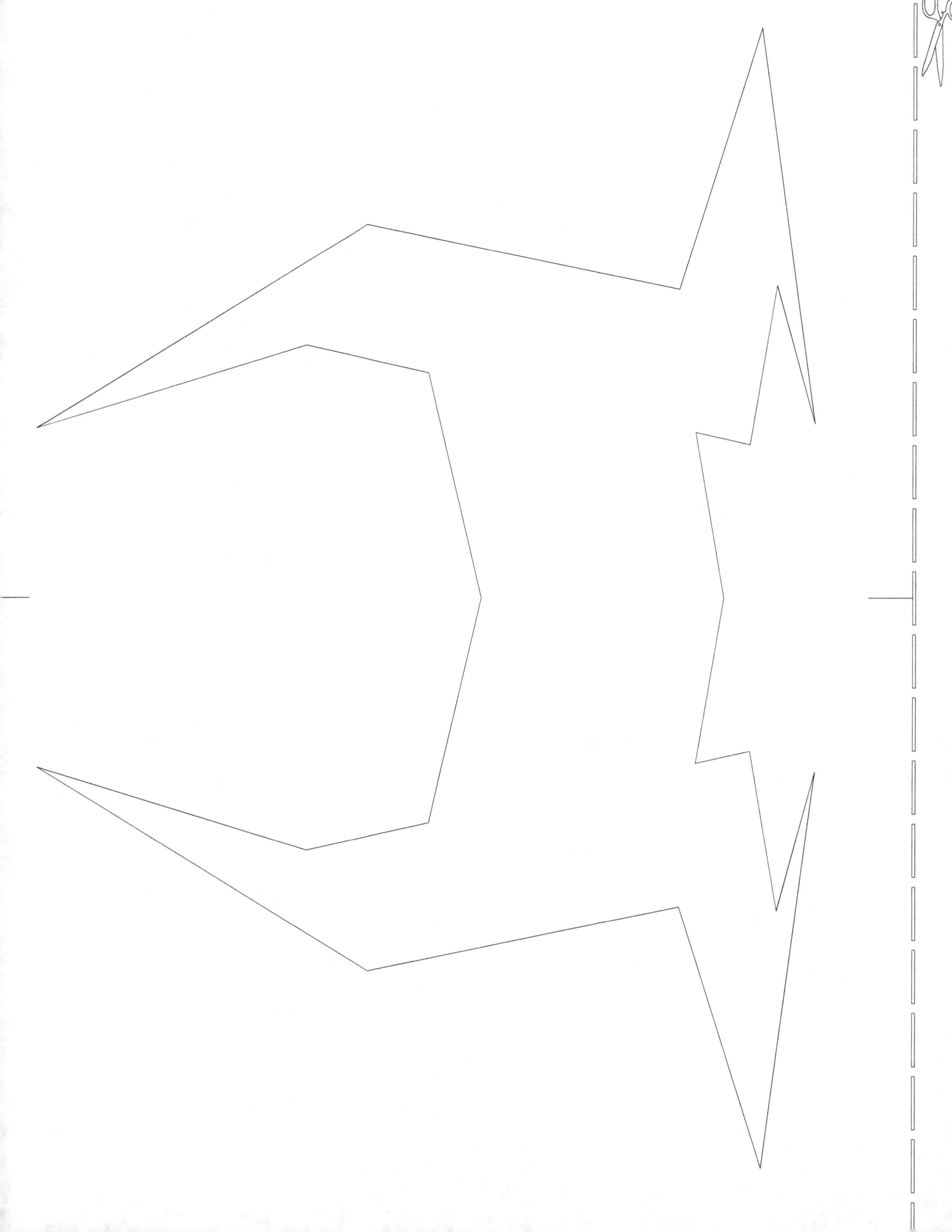

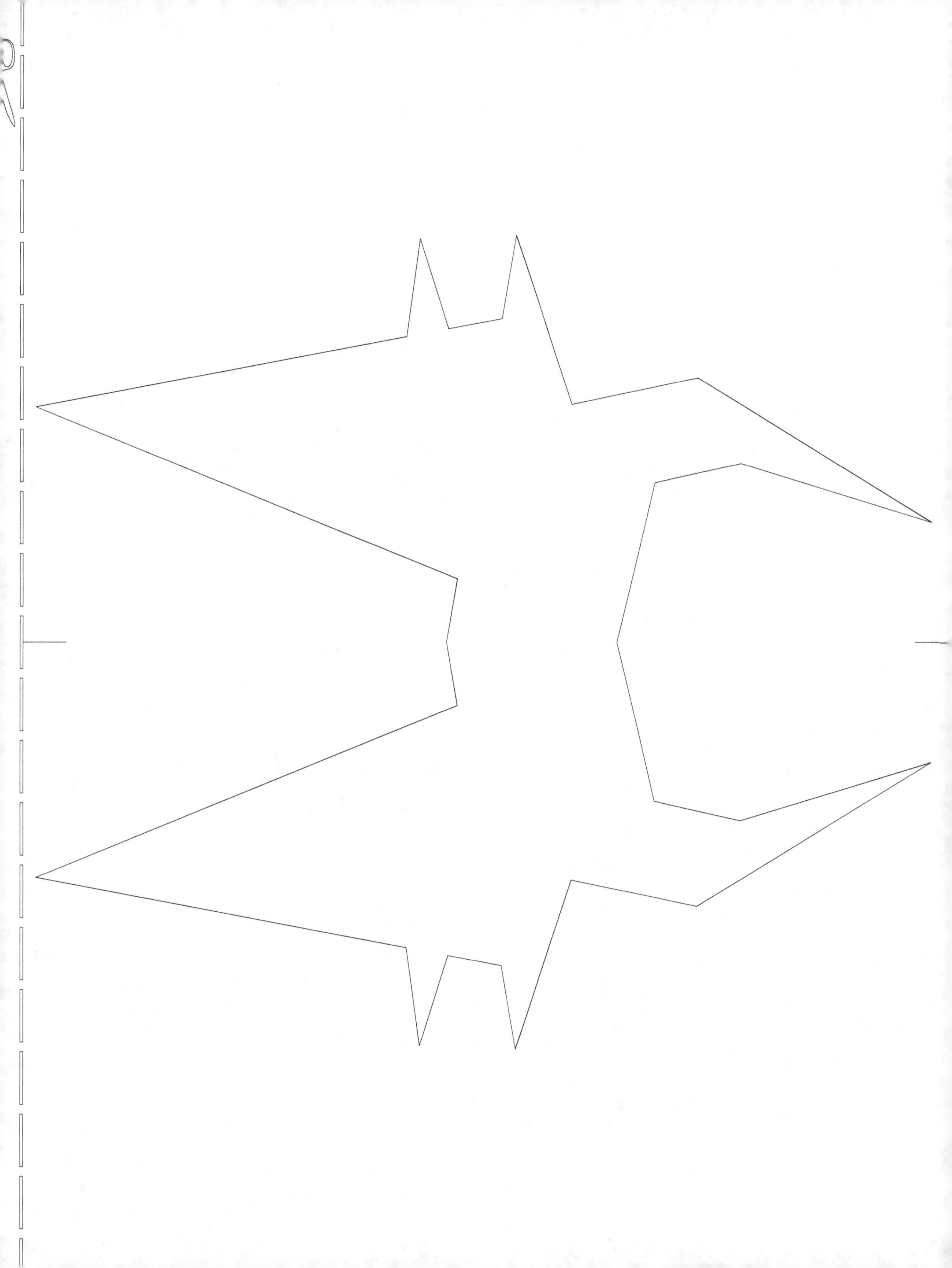

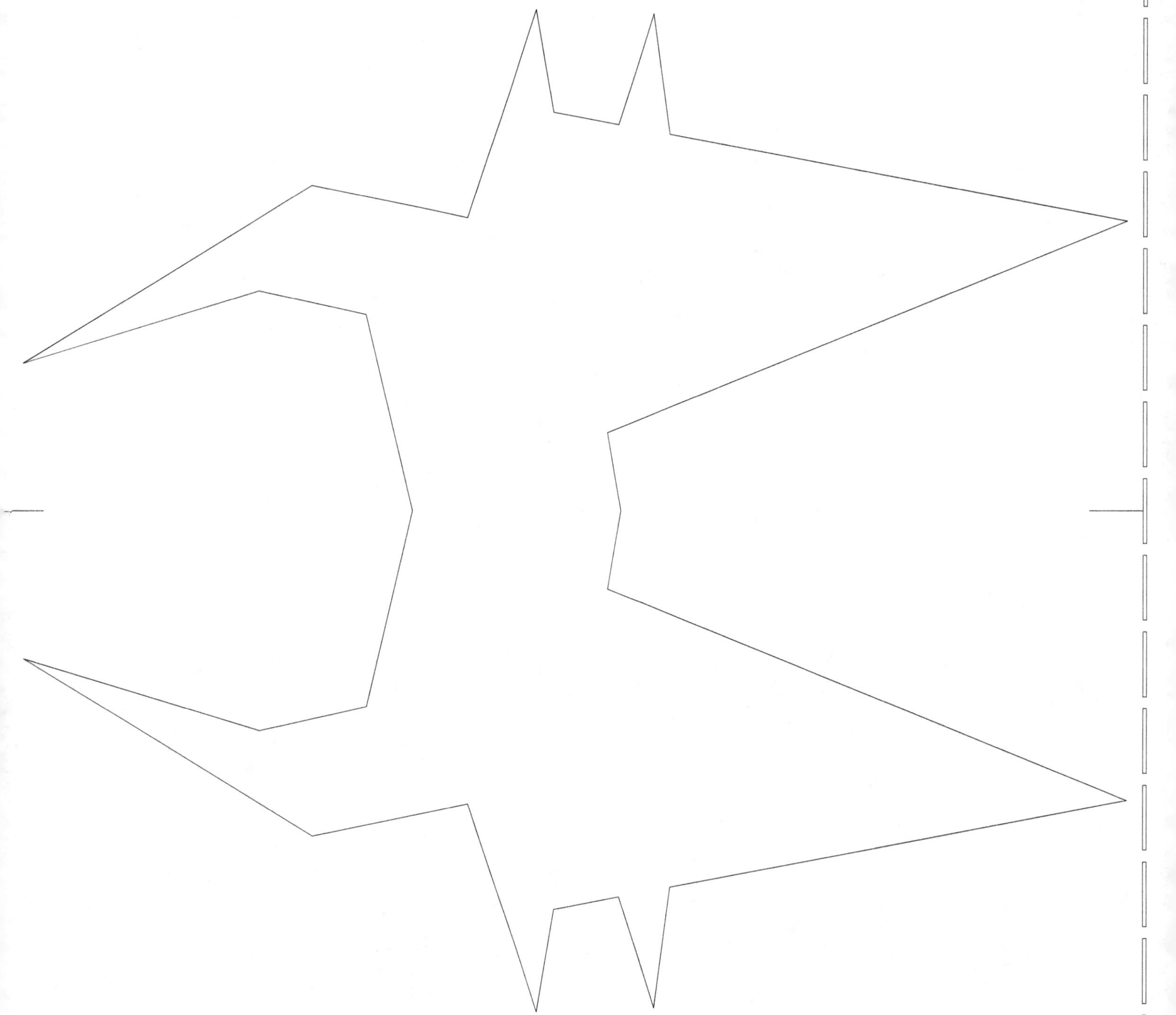

www.ingramcontent.com/pod-product-compliance
Lightning Source LLC
Chambersburg PA
CBHW080853170526
45158CB00009B/2723
* 9 7 8 0 9 9 9 5 3 4 3 3 5 *